W9-BXQ-352

Defender of America's Gulf Coast

A History of Ellington Field, Texas

1917-2007

Kathryn Black Morrow

Kathryn Black Morrow, M.A.

Morrow House Publishing
Houston, Texas
2007

Morrow House Publishing
P.O. Box 58485
Houston, TX 77258
281-461-4819
kathrynmorrowresearch@att.net

www.KathrynMorrowResearch.com

ISBN# — 978-0-9796870-0-6
LOC# — 2007936729

Morrow, Kathryn Black.
Defender of America's Gulf Coast, a history of Ellington Field, Texas 1917-2007 / Kathryn Black Morrow.
p. cm.
Includes bibliographical references and index.
ISBN 978-0-9796870-0-6
1. Ellington Field (Texas)--History. 2. Texas--History, Military. 3. United States. Army Air Forces--History. 4. United States--Armed Forces--Women--History. 5. African American Soldiers--History. I. Title.

U294.5.E3 M67 2007
355.00976420—dc22 2007936729

Production Team
Rita Mills of The Book Connection — Project Manager
www.BookConnectionOnline.com
Deborah Frontiera — Line Editing
Victor Higginbotham — Cover Design

The paper used in this publication meets the requirements of the American National Standard for Permanence of Paper for Printed Library Materials Z39.48-1984.

Printed in the United States of America

Table of Contents

Acknowledgements

This book could not have been written without the help and guidance of many people. My grateful thanks go to all the men and women who took the time to talk to me, especially those people who read the manuscript in its various stages and encouraged me to finish it. I say thank you to the "Ace in the Hole" group, the "Gathering of Eagles" group, and the wonderful men who called themselves my OADGs—my "Old As Dirt Guys," whose memory for details and suggestions often led me to new sources for primary source information. A special posthumous thank you to Rev. Snowden McKinnon, whose interviews opened up the experiences of the African American soldiers of the 79th Aviation Squadron at Ellington field in an era before integration. My thanks also goes to the women of Ellington Field; the WAACs, WACs and WOOFTDs who worked as nurses, "Plane Janes" or ferry pilots during World War II, and those who became astronaut trainers and astronauts during the modern era. They shared many personal experiences and photos with me. Marlene Champion, a long-time antique dealer in Houston, allowed me to use part of her collection of unpublished original photographs taken by the photographer for the book, *Ellington 1918*.

No researcher could accomplish anything without the frequent and diligent help of librarians. I was generously assisted by the staff at the Texas Room of the Houston Public Library and the University of Houston Clear Lake, Johnson Space Center collection, among many others. My foundation research was done in the JSC collection, where archivist Shelly Kelly never flinched when I asked for a copy every reference to Ellington Field.

She also read and commented on the original master's thesis and several revisions of chapters in this book.

Col. Lanny McNeely, commander of the 147th Fighter Interceptor Group at Ellington Field, and his Executive Secretary Ms. Margaret Henson, gave me open access to the Base Historian's office, and always treated me with great courtesy and professionalism. We stood shoulder to shoulder in the fight to keep the 147th FIG at Ellington during the Base Realignment and Closure process, but it was a battle we lost. Another ally in a battle lost was Vietnam veteran Malcolm Browne, who asked me to join him in an effort to build a national Veterans Museum on vacant land at Ellington Field. The museum will be built, but not at Ellington Field. Mr. Browne opened many doors for me in my research on Ellington, and I am grateful.

My biggest thanks, of course, goes to my long-suffering husband, Mike, who for three years put up with a wife who spent days wandering around the house talking to herself when she was trying to compose just the right paragraph, and whose mind often in dwelt in another era of history. He was always my first editor and my chief consultant, and will always be my sweetheart. My cousin Marilyn Lewis, an editor and author in her own right, was an early reviewer of the manuscript. Additional family support came from my two sisters, who always expected great things from me, and my four children, who are all married with children of their own. They never doubted that I could get this book done, even when I had decided it would never be good enough to be published. To these few mentioned, and to all the many people who in one way or another said "Yes, you can," I hope your faith in me has been rewarded.

Introduction

Ellington Field was one of many military bases in the United States that were catapulted into existence by the threat of a global war, in this case, World War I. Like many of the other bases, Ellington was built up and then largely abandoned once the threat of war was past. Unlike other bases, Ellington Field survived not only the first closing after World War I, but several re-openings and closings over the ninety years of its existence. Ellington Field is the only base I have discovered that has been closed and then reactivated so many times. The repeated re-openings point to the fact that Ellington's location remained strategically important to the defense of Texas and the gulf coast over time, and that its modern mission, especially Ellington's part in the Space program, is still critical today. Almost every aspect of the development of military aviation, from the beginning of flight to the Space Shuttle, happened during the history of Ellington Field. It holds a unique place in the history of military aviation in the United States.

The history of Ellington Field is a microcosm of the military history of the United States for the entire 20th century, and continues into the twenty-first century. The opening, closing, and reopening of Ellington also reflected the shifts in national attitude toward the military and the place of the United States of America in the world community. The lives and the character of those who served at Ellington Field revealed, sometimes poignantly, their simple dedication and contribution to the national and world events which they shaped and which shaped them. History is a record of the results of the decisions and actions of individual people, Some people are called on to lead and others are called on to contribute to the unfolding of events in quiet but essential ways. The people who worked and trained at Ellington Field provided thousands of fine examples that illustrated the importance of the character of the individual to this particular military facility and the surrounding community, our nation, and on occasion, the free world.

This history is built on reams of documents, months of reading and years of research, but it was the personal stories of the men and women at Ellington that I found the most interesting. I have selected a few of the most relevant to highlight the history, but there were so many it was a constant battle for me to stay focused on the stories and events which pertained to the history of Ellington, and not be pulled too far away from my subject into the story of the Space Center, the effects of military service on families and communities, the issues of segregation and desegregation, or other larger topics.

One of the stories that revealed itself to me came when I was sorting through my father's military papers. I was born in Houston, not far from Ellington Air Force Base, and grew up as a military brat, the daughter of Air Force Reserve officer Col. Kermit K. Black. The timeline of his career mirrored the first thirty-nine years of Ellington Field's, from his enlistment in 1924 to his retirement in Wiesbaden, Germany in 1963. (See Biography Section). He began his military career when he was still in high school in Tampa, Florida. In January of 1924, he enlisted in the 116th Horse Drawn Field Artillery Unit of the Florida National Guard and subsequently served in the Reserve Officers Training Corps (R.O.T.C) at the University of Florida. He continued to serve in the Army Infantry Reserve, Civilian Conservation Corps (C.C.C.), the Coast Artillery Reserve, and the United States Air Force. One of his assignments was as the Commander of an Air Force Reserve unit, the 158th Aircraft Control and Warning Group, at Ellington Air Force Base in 1951. My father's personal connection with Ellington combined with Ellington's essential role in the history of military aviation, two world wars, and the history of the Air Force, made writing a history of Ellington Field an irresistible subject for my research.

Most military histories written in the twentieth century, the time period of this book, concentrated on the techniques of wars and campaigns, or the biographies of the leaders involved. Few delved into the history of the military bases the men served on. According to Yvonne Kincaid of the Air Force History Department at the Pentagon,[1] "After World War II no base histories were written. Actually there was never a requirement to write base histories as such.... After World War II histories are of the squadrons, groups, and other organizations assigned to the base." Ellington Field was one base that did weave a little history into its military organizational summaries.

Sources for the early history of Ellington Field were very few, but they were rich in detail and personal commentary. The first yearbook, *Ellington 1918*, was a primary source of information, and usually the only source used for most articles written on the 1917-1920 period of Ellington Field history. Archived copies of the 1918 weekly post newspaper, "Tale Spins," yielded more details about the soldiers' lives during World War I. Letters written by Aviation Cadet Ira B. McNair, who was stationed at Ellington Field in 1918, were sent to me in 2003, and some of that material was incorporated into this book. The other major source of information on the progress in Ellington Field history through the early years was newspaper articles.

There was much more material available for the World War II period. Several military reports on Ellington Field exist for isolated years on three rolls of microfilm at the Air Force History and Research Agency located on Maxwell Air Force Base in Montgomery, Alabama, and there are numerous newspapers *The Houston Post, Houston Press, LaPorte Liberator, Houston Informer*, the National Guard newspaper, *The Skylander*, and others. The National Aeronautic and Space Administration (NASA) had a monthly newspaper called *Space News Roundup*, which was a wealth of information for the period of 1962-2005. In 1999, NASA employee Erik Carlson wrote an excellent paper titled *Ellington 1918-1963*. In 2003, Dr. Carlson invited me to come to the archives at the University of Texas at Dallas, gave me some valuable advice about sources and publishing, and directed me to several more books that included information on Ellington Field and military aviation in Texas.

During my three years of research, I found no other airfields that rebounded from as many closings as Ellington Field. Since the little airfield lasted through several presidencies and weathered the changing winds of political expediencies, its continual rebirth and survival could not have been based solely on political pork barreling or favoritism. Ellington was simply the right base in the right place during all the needful times.

Since Ellington Field's existence spanned the entire period of military aviation development from its beginning to the Space Program, through more than eight decades of United States history, its history offers a unique view of national issues like segregation, desegregation, women's pre- and post war roles, women in the military, the effect of military service on families, and the impact of a military base on the local community. Writing a history needs no further justification than the need to record information for posterity, and since Ellington Field has been a part of local, state and national history for eighty-five years, its history definitely deserves a place on the library shelves. Ellington Field played a vital role in World War I by training America's young men to fly. In World War II, the base was re-opened to train young men as pilots, bombardiers, navigators and aerial gunners. By the end of World War II, a new social imperative no longer limited military training to men. In 1943, Ellington Field graduated the first class of women pilots in an era when few people thought women could fly airplanes. From 1959 to the year 2000, Johnson Space Center in Houston had trained 321 NASA astronauts, 45 of whom were women.[2] Whether pilots or mission specialists, they all trained at Ellington Field.[3],[4]

More recently, after the terrorist attack of September 11, 2001, Ellington's military presence continued to be relevant when the Texas National Guard, the Texas Air National Guard, and the Coast Guard units that occupy space at Ellington Field acted as first responders and a major deterrent in the defense of the nation's petrochemical industry located all along the Gulf Coast. In 2005, future plans for Ellington Field included making it a "Joint Forces Base", by moving Army Reserve Units to the base, and there are plans to open a regional office for Homeland Security at the field (see Chapter Five). When the jets from Ellington fly over my house, I never complain about the noise.

End Notes

[1] Yvonne Kincaid, email response, Yvonne.Kincaid@pentagon.af.mil, accessed 12/7/2001.

[2] *Astronaut Program-Applications Chart*, also *Minority and Women Astronauts Selected-Through 2000 Chart,43 Women(Includes Minorities),32 Minorities (Includes 8 Women),* NASA Public Relations Department, 2003.

[3] Duane Ross, Manager for Astronaut Candidate Selection and Training, Interview by telephone, NASA Public Relations Department, 2003, information updated May 11, 2005.

[4] Except the "Mercury 13" women and others, whose testing in 1961 predated the move to Texas and Ellington Field.

Defender of America's Gulf Coast

A History of Ellington Field, Texas

1917-2007

CHAPTER I

Ellington Field 1917 to World War II

Ellington Field is one of the oldest and most significant sites in the history of military aviation in the United States. It is located between the southernmost edge of Houston, Texas, and the site of NASA's (National Aeronautics and Space Administration) Johnson Space Center. The location is symbolic of its connection both to the past and the future of Texas. The history of Ellington Field, later to become Ellington Air Force Base, often paralleled the boom-and-bust cycle of the history of Houston and Texas itself. Just as the opening of a military base was often a boon to local economies, the closing of a military base often constituted a deathblow. Bases that were closed were seldom reopened. Ellington Field, however, has survived multiple closings, only to re-emerge, phoenix-like, each time the security of the United States was in jeopardy.

Construction of the airfield began in September of 1917, and Ellington Field quickly rose from an inglorious beginning as a swampy cow pasture to become the heart of the largest aviation training program in the fledgling Army Air Service. Ellington was a major link between the development of civilian uses of aviation in the United States, and the application of military air power in wartime. [1]

Many of the "firsts" in aviation invention and development, from the earliest stages of flight to the Space Age, were made by the men at Ellington Field. It became one of the largest aviation training bases in the nation during two World Wars,[2] and for ninety years, it has continued to train men and women through the Korean War, the Persian Gulf War and the war with Iraq.

Ellington Field remained a vital link in the aviation industry in Texas. The tenants at Ellington have changed over the years, but Ellington continued. It served as a satellite airport for Continental Airlines, a base for the Texas Air National Guard, Texas Army National Guard, and the Coast Guard, and an auxiliary-training field for NASA astronauts. Over its many years of service, visiting dignitaries from presidents to potentates made Ellington Field their arrival airport of choice, because its size and ever-present military reserve strength made it much more secure for landings and take-offs.[3] Ellington's strategic location played a vital role in the defense of the Texas Gulf Coast's petrochemical and aerospace industries and recently made this airfield an important base of operations for the nation's newly organized, anti-terrorist Department of Homeland Security defense system.

Ellington Fiekd, Texas 1918 from Ellington 1918

The site was named for Lt. Eric Lamar Ellington (1889-1913), who was one of the early casualties of the air service. Lt. Ellington, a 1909 graduate of the U.S. Naval Academy, transferred to the U.S. Army in 1911 to pursue his interest in aeronautical science.[4] He was assigned first to Fort Sam Houston, Texas, and then transferred to the Aeronautical Division of the U.S. Army Signal Corps in College Park, Maryland. He qualified as a military aviator on August 11, 1913. After three short months of training with the 1st Aero Squadron aviation school in Texas City, Texas, Lt. Ellington was assigned to the U.S. Army Signal Corps aviation school on North Island, near San Diego, California.[5] On November 24, 1913, the young Lieutenant was on a training mission with student co-pilot Lt. Hugh Kelly (1881-1913). Lt. Ellington and Lt. Kelly were both killed when their plane nose-dived into the landing field.

Ellington Field Barracks Courtesy Marlene Champion Collection

It is likely that during his aviation training at Texas City, Texas, the 24-year-old Ellington flew over the area that would one day bear his name. In an article commemorating the 70th anniversary of the opening of Ellington Field, Jim Higgins, the director of public information at the College of the Mainland in Texas City, observed, "If he could have seen into the future, he would have been astonished to learn that there would one day be an Ellington Field down there, a place where pilots, bombardiers and navigators would be trained for two world wars, where presidents and heads of state would touch down on visits to Houston, where moon-bound astronauts and shuttle crews would train. But from 1,000 feet up in the spring of 1913, it didn't look like much."[6]

At the end of 1916, the United States had only 12 qualified military pilots, one of whom, Lt. Col. Ira A. Rader (1887-1958)[7], would become Ellington Field's fourth Commanding Officer in 1918. At the time of America's declaration of war against Germany on April 6, 1917, the development of aviation in the United States had barely begun. The Aeronautical Division of the Signal corps was only nine years old.[8] The newly formed Aviation Section of the U.S. Army Signal Corps could only look with envy at the air war being fought in Europe, where French and British pilots were flying high as commanders of the sky. In June of 1918, ninety three aviation personnel were sent overseas to study French and British airplanes and manufacturing methods, and then bring those skills back to the United States.[9] The U.S. aircraft manufacturing industry was in its infancy, and the entire U.S. aviation fleet totaled only 250 airplanes plus five balloons.[10]

When the U.S entered World War I, it had no military air arm capable of fighting an enemy. It did, however, have an untapped pool of men and materials to offer. England and France, almost completely depleted of both men and materials, after years of war, looked hopefully towards America's strength.[11]

On January 24, 1917, French Premier Alexandre Ribot asked the United States to contribute 4,500 airplanes, 5,000 pilots and 50,000 mechanics to the war effort by the spring of 1918.[12] It was an enormous task. With more enthusiasm than wisdom, the United States Congress agreed and appropriated $640 million dollars for aeronautics and the production of training airplanes.[13] By the end of World War I in 1918, more than 9,000 military pilots had qualified for service as well as the many navigators, bombardiers, aerial gunners, and radio operators needed to support them. A large number of these men were trained at Ellington Field.[14]

Convinced by the success of the French and British experiences with an air war, the government of the United States appropriated funding to establish a new Air Service as part of the old Signal Corps. The Signal Corps quickly scouted good locations, drew up plans for airfields, ordered supplies and brought over the most famous French and British instructors to train some of the best and brightest of the nation's young men to fly.

Flying was a dangerous, learn-as-you-go experiment at this early point in its development. Young pilots like Eric Ellington and Hugh Kelly took off in fragile airplanes with as yet unproven engines, unknown design capabilities and still-evolving flying techniques. Many attempts at takeoffs and landings ended in wrecks. Minutes in the air required hours in the shop.[15] The new Air Service looked for locations with mild weather the year around, unimpeded visibility, and a terrain free of natural obstacles to use for its airfields. The fewer obstacles the inexperienced pilots could possibly fly into, the better. The flat, almost treeless coastal plains of south Texas were ideal for the purposes of the Air Service.

The original training programs included schools for pilots, bombardiers, aerial gunners, and radio operators. Graduates expected assignments to combat posts in Europe during World War I. By the end of the war in November of 1918, Ellington housed 5,000 men and 250 aircraft, and had a reputation as one of the best-equipped and most complete flying schools in the country. The transfer of the thousands of Ellington Field's aviation trainees to bases all over the United States and to units in Europe spread Ellington's reputation as a premier site for training aviators in the United States. Aviators and officers visiting from overseas thought the program at Ellington excelled that of any training school in Europe.[16]

City officials, local politicians and the Houston Chamber of Commerce foresaw the tremendous economic boost a huge military training base would bring to Houston. They worked together to push for the completion of the base. At one point, when labor difficulties stopped the construction completely, they ordered two companies of infantry from Camp Logan to be sent to enforce the settlement of labor strikes.[17]

Construction on the 1,280-acre site at Ellington Field began September 14, 1917, and within two months the aircraft hangars and runways were built. The first detachment of troops arrived on November 10 from the 120th Squadron at Kelly Field in San Antonio, Texas. Most of the men in this first detachment were mechanics, or "mechnicians", as they were called then. It is important to realize that just as there were few airplanes built by 1917, there were even fewer mechanics who knew how to build, repair or maintain them. The War Department manual on the care and overhauling of airplane engines explained where these mechanics would come from:

> In the case of the mechanicians, the object will be to make an airplane motor man out of an automobile mechanic or machinist. Parts of it (the course, ed.) should be given to automobile factories to help them train aviation mechanics....In the case of student flyers, it is to give them a practical knowledge of airplane motors sufficient to enable them to diagnose motor trouble when on cross-country flights and to make rapid and practical repairs if possible, or, in any event, to be able to send an intelligent message for parts, etc....[18]

The mechanics immediately began assembling airplanes from the stacks of parts piled in the newly-built hangars. Working every day from reveille to taps, the mechanics had the first airplane assembled, tested and ready to fly by November 27, 1917. On that Thanksgiving Day, as the first plane roared up from the freshly finished runway, a new military aviation tradition began at Ellington Field.[18]

Ellington Field Mechanics Shop, Courtesy Marlene Champion Collection

In the rush to assemble enough airplanes to keep the pilot trainees in the air, building housing for the men received considerably less attention than building hangars to house the planes. Lt. G. S. Voorhees, one of the first flying cadets in 1917, stated in an interview many years later:

> We didn't live in barracks. We lived in tents—five of us to a tent. The tents were pretty wet and soggy.... The ground was wet and soggy. The drainage was bad. Sometimes there were days at a time when the planes couldn't get out of the mud and into the air. Whenever we got any time off, we tore into town-either Houston or Galveston.[19]

Up to this point in aviation history, navigation from the air meant visually recognizing local landmarks like rivers, roadways and cities. Pilots simply looked over the side of the airplane to see where they were. Flying at a high altitude, at night or in foul weather obstructed the view of the landmarks on the ground. At Ellington Field, a newly developed course called Aerial Navigation taught student pilots how to fly from place to place without reference to the ground. Pilots could then confidently navigate from place to place without being able to see any landmarks below. This represented a major leap forward from instructing students to fly to the red water tower and turn right, or follow the coastline and keep the Gulf of Mexico on their left.

Soldiers Tents and Dining Hall from Ellington 1918

Early training flights were necessarily short due to limitations on fuel capacity and pilot fatigue. Aviation cadet Ira B. McNair, wrote in a letter dated October 1, 1918; "We flew to a place called Richmond, Texas, did not land but 'jazzed' around over the city…. My pilot did nose dives, vertical banks and side slips until the town looked as if it were where the moon ought to be…I took a picture of the city while the pilot very obligingly turned the ship on its nose, so I could get it without the wires being in! (Support wires of the wings)…It was so bumpy at 2000 feet that it was like riding a flat-tired Ford over the cobblestones, only the bumps were big! Down we'd go and then jump way up again! Every time we went over a railroad or Macadam road, we would scoot way up and slide down on the other side. The heated air currents…do it."[20]

Handley-Page Airplane, Ellington Field from the book, Ellington 1918

Graduates from Ellington's training courses excelled in the long cross-country flights that were an international rage during that era, as well. Lt. Erik H. Nelson (1888-1970), an Ellington graduate, participated in the 1919 Gulf to Pacific flight. During his career he gained more cross-country experience than any other officer in the Air Service. His courage and skill later earned him a coveted place in the first round-the-world flight held in 1924.[21] The June 20, 1919 edition of *Tale Spins*, the post newspaper, proudly carried the headline: "Two Handley-Pages Complete Flight from Elizabeth,

New Jersey, to Ellington Field—Lack of Proper Landing Fields Hinder Flight, but an Average Air Speed of Over Eighty Miles per Hour is Maintained."[22] Eighty miles an hour is not fast by modern speed standards, but it was twice the average speed of the first "heavier-than-air flying machine" the Wright Brothers had delivered to the U.S. Army Signal Corps just eleven years earlier, and quite an achievement for the times.[23]

Navigation school students learned the constellations, compass reading, and the art of celestial navigation. With the limited ground-to-air communication of the era, flying at night required advanced navigational skills and a good sense of direction and speed. Ellington Field and the surrounding coastal plain were frequently subject to cloudy weather, and flying at night was an even more dangerous proposition. Flying Cadet Granville Gutterson[24] described flying on a foggy night this way:

> Sometimes we have a fog which makes it bad for night flying. It is pretty lonesome work, especially when the fog obstructs the lights from all the farms below.... If they go out because of the fog...you're out of luck. All you run your ship by is the 'feel', for it is pitch black all around.... If you get above the fog you are liable to lose yourself and then...you begin to think what a darn little thing your existence is, compared to the universe in general.... You dive down, about one thousand feet...watch your altimeter so that you don't go too low, and then bank, first one way and then another, and look and hunt for the glow through the fog which indicates home...You've got gas enough for a half hour more...and a lot of things can happen in that time.... The fog can blow away or you can fly out over the ocean, or your engine might fail or get on fire, or the ship tail-spin or a dozen other things...Then you see a glow way off to the left and you point to it and the ship comes around with a bank that almost pushes you through the seat and you dive toward home!...You unfasten the straps and don't say a darn word but walk over to the fire where the other fellows are and you notice the ambulance is gone, and two crews are missing...you lie down on your coat beside the fire and wait for the fog to clear up and try it again.[25]

Engineers at Ellington Field magnified the power of the limelight, also called calcium light, that was used to light stages and theaters to a new military application. The light was produced by heating lime to incandescence. The resulting intensely white and bright light was then focused on the sky through a lens.[26] The powerful beacon of the calcium light lit up the runway and made it possible for planes to take off and land on the darkest night.

The instrumentation on the Curtiss O.X. training planes was originally limited to clocks and compasses. As navigational instruments improved, night flying became just another daring adventure for the young pilots. The advent of the calcium light meant that day or night, in cloudy skies or clear, Ellington pilots could take off, turn left at the North Star, and head confidently into the sky.

Night Flying from, Ellington 1918

Instructors in the second school at Ellington Field taught aerial bombing techniques. Ellington was the only bombardier training school in the nation with complete night and day bombing courses. The bombing range, just east of the main airfield, had a huge bullseye at its center. When the bombardier hit the bullseye during the day, a puff of smoke was released to give the pilot and bombardier a visual indication of an on-target hit. At night, a direct hit produced a flash of light. Mechanics adapted the planes for bombardier training by tacking racks loaded with dummy bombs onto the plane's belly. Coordination between bombardiers and the pilots gradually improved so that practice-bombing runs ceased to menace local houses and cows, and became more accurate more often. By the end of 1918, Ellington bombardiers could hit a target on the ground from 9,000 feet with remarkable regularity.[27]

Aerial Gunnery, from Ellington 1918

Pilots had to learn to do more than just fly an airplane. In combat, many instructors considered aerial gunnery accuracy more important than flying. Reports coming back from the war overseas proved that a pilot's gunnery skills often made the difference between his coming home alive or becoming a tragic statistic. Flying Cadets received a basic course in gunnery and weapons familiarity at ground schools. At advanced flying schools like Ellington, instructors concentrated on the use of machine guns and taught the students everything they would need to know about aircraft weaponry and synchronized firing at firing ranges. Combat aerial gunnery in airplanes was done out over the ocean from a range in nearby San Leon. Only after intensive preparation were the students ready for combat target firing. Aerial gunnery work was the finishing touch in their preparation for combat flying.[28]

Aerial Gunnery, from Ellington 1918

The Aerial Gunnery School[29] at San Leon, Texas, was located about half a mile inland from Galveston Bay and about twelve feet above sea level. It was a largely unpopulated rural area, with herds of horses and cattle roaming freely. The students lived in tents with no floors. When it rained, as it often did, the tents blew down and were swamped with water. The location was too rural to have electricity, so there were no lighting facilities. When it got dark, the men had no choice but to gather around a fire or go to bed. Drinking water had to be hauled by truck from town seven miles away, and after a heavy storm, when the dirt roads be came impassable, the men might go thirty-six hours without water. Gunnery students at San Leon learned a lotabout the local wildlife- it was necessary to shake them out of every item of clothing before putting it on. Scorpions, tarantulas, centipedes, lizards and snakes crawled into the tents during the night. The presence of the numerous cattle brought hordes of flies. Recreation was limited, because it was a seven mile walk to the nearest town. Swimming in the warm, shallow waters of the bay was a relief for some, but the soldiers had to be careful because the deep troughs between the sand bars were used by large sharks as corrals for schools of fish they were chasing for dinner. The soldiers found it necessary to post a "watcher" on the beach. [30]

Flight instructors made use of the latest advances in ground-to-air communication and communications within the aircraft. In the earliest days of flying, once pilots took off there was no way for their instructors to communicate with them from the ground. Flight instructors who accompanied students on training flights simply shouted directions from the back seat to the student in the front seat. Open cockpits required instructors to yell their orders against the rushing wind and over the sound of the engine noise. By the end of 1918, however, it had become possible for student pilots to receive instant instruction by radiotelephone from their instructors, an advance that dramatically improved the coordination of flight positioning and maneuvers. The Radio Department at Ellington Field was established in January 1918, and further improvements in wireless communication enabled personnel on the ground to listen to and join in on conversations with pilots in the air, even when their planes were miles away.[31]

Aerial View of San Leon, Texas from, Ellington 1918

The field of aviation was so new to the military that its first pilots were civilians who had learned what they knew on their own. The excellence of the training program at Ellington and the dedication of its officers attracted many top-notch civilian instructors. One was Harry B. Crewdson (1882-1956),[32] then considered the "Dean" of flying, who was one of fewer than a dozen civilian pilots who had flown for more than seven years and was still alive to tell about it. At Ellington Field, he taught the first course in military formation flying offered anywhere in the country. Orton B. Hoover

(1889-1958), the father of the Brazilian naval air service, served as the first instructor of night-flying training at Ellington.

Everything about flying was also new to most Houstonians, and people were intensely curious about the military "city" that had sprung up in the middle of a cow pasture between Houston and Galveston. Excited throngs of people attended every open house at the airfield, eager to take a look at the new-fangled flying machines lined up on the runways and ponder how such aircraft could fly. When the first mass formation flight took off from Ellington on December 5th 1918, the citizens of Houston poured into the streets, their eyes focused on a sky now darkened with hundreds of planes that thundered overhead, their shadows passing over the upturned faces of the crowd as if giving their benediction to the end of the war. The flying demonstration was made to benefit the Red Cross Drive in Houston. Local factories sounded their sirens, and fire stations rang their bells in response as the planes came into view over the city and dropped thousands of Red Cross leaflets to the crowds of people below.[33]

Ellington Field Aircraft, World War I, from Ellington 1918

Ellington Field, populated by several thousand crisply uniformed single men, was also an exciting addition to the local society, especially for the young ladies. Handsome pilots flying through the night in their gossamer aircraft made an irresistibly romantic picture. Dances and soirées were held on base at regular intervals, making Ellington Field a popular rendezvous. Names preceded by a military rank soon began appearing in the society columns and marriage records. Articles about adventures and misadventures at Ellington Field filled the local newspapers each week.

As mentioned previously, many of the heroes of aviation history came to Houston to be instructors or to be trained at Ellington Field during their careers. These officers and men carried innovations and ideas they learned from hands-on experience at Ellington to other fields and into other training programs. These new ideas and developments in aviation technology brought national recognition to Ellington and Houston. [34] Some of the recorded "firsts" at Ellington came about simply because Ellington was one of the first advanced flight, bombing, and navigation schools in the nation to offer those courses. By default it was the first field to execute a three-day bombing run, the first to offer training in formation flying, and the first to establish an aerial gunnery range because it was one of the first schools. Other achievements, such as being the first field in the South to receive the British-made DeHavilland 4-B planes installed with the newest American-made "Liberty" motor in 1918, were more the luck of the draw. The planes were used for bombing practice runs, but reached the U.S. troops too late to be used in combat during World War I. This fact may have given comfort later to pilot trainees when the DeHaviland earned the deadly nickname, the "Flying Coffin."[35] Nevertheless, Ellington earned an international reputation as a top-notch flying training school in part because of the development of these aviation "firsts" and the expertise of its instructors. The airfield was the first to take up cross-country flights, and Ellington students successfully flew to airfields as far away as Michigan, Colorado and Washington, D.C. It was also the first to develop an aerial gunnery range with moving targets. Engineers at Ellington expanded night flying by developing the use of the calcium light.[36]

Major Robert B. Hunter, flight surgeon at Ellington Field, explained an interesting example of how one of the "firsts" in aviation invention was made at Ellington:

> It was only a few months ago that the idea of transporting injured men by airplane was conceived and tried out at Ellington. A Curtiss JN4 training plane with a 150-horsepower Hispano-Suiza motor was selected for the experiment. The cowl in front of the rear cockpit and two feet of fuselage covering behind it were made

> removable, as well as the rear seat. The floor of the body was built to accommodate a regulation army stretcher, which can be made fast to the floor of the fuselage to keep it from coming out of place in banking or gliding. The patient is kept from sliding off the stretcher by broad bands around his ankles, his waist and his chest... The ship has been coated with white enamel with red crosses on the wings, instead of the usual insignia, and upon each side of the body. The success of the aerial ambulance plan here has led to its adoption at many other flying fields....[37]

More records were set when Ellington became the first post to publish a regular camp paper, titled *Tale Spins*, and Ellington was also the first military post to introduce the "girl canteen workers," and innovation which blazed the way for the USO workers who came later. [38]

At the height of production, airfields like Ellington housed large assembly facilities where airplanes were assembled from parts that arrived fresh from the factory in boxes. Material shortages were common, and parts were often salvaged from other equipment. Lt. Garrett H. Graham, a reporter for the base newspaper *Tale Spins*, explained about efficiency at Ellington:

> In another instance, the engineering department was short of wristpins with which to repair Curtiss motors. Instead of allowing the planes to stand idle, and the men to twiddle their thumbs while waiting for the spare parts to arrive from the factory, someone had a bright idea and purchased some broken axles from Ford cars at a salvage shop. The axles were cut into the proper lengths, specially treated and used as wrist pins. They filled the purpose admirably and no difference could be noted between them and the genuine article.[39]

This quote emphasized that the Ellington Field supply system expected results, and not excuses: "Adaptability and originality were prized above a religious adherence to moth-eaten rules and customs."[40] Using salvaged auto parts seems reckless by modern safety standards, but viewed within the context of the "keep them flying" credo of the Air Service, and the "waste not" philosophy of a wartime and post-depression U.S. economy, it was understandable. Furthermore, since airplane mechanics were mostly retrained automobile mechanics, they were adapting parts with which they were experienced and which they understood.

The "Angel of Meraj" ambulance plane taken from Ellington 1918

Keeping the airplanes in good shape was not a haphazard process. Pilots had a checklist that they completed before and after each flight, and engineers checked each plane over every night in the hangars. Mechanics overhauled the engines on a regular basis, and assembled and thoroughly tested each part on new planes before they were turned over to the pilots.[41]

All of the inventions and improvements in maintenance and techniques did not alter the fact that the Air Service, in its infancy, was a deadly assignment. Military combat planes in this decade were built from wood and fabric or lightweight metal and wire. They were fragile and often temperamental. Newly developed and little tested engines were mounted into these shells. The glamour of the flyboys dimmed by the end of World War I, when one observer estimated that the number of deaths in the Army Air Service was *4,200% higher* than the average for all the other army branches combined. In 1921, for instance, 92% of the accidental deaths in the army occurred in the Air Service alone.[42] The first death at Ellington occurred on December 31, 1917, when Sgt. Sam Norvick, a machinist with the 191st Aero Squadron was struck by a whirring propeller blade and killed.[43] The first air casualty occurred January 16, 1918 when pilot Gerald V. Carroll lost control of his biplane during a formation flight and spiraled 5,000 feet to the ground near South Houston. The accident came just three hours after Ellington Field Base Commander Col. John Curry gave a talk to the Houston Chamber of Commerce on airplane navigation safety.[44] The total number of deaths at Ellington Field in 1917/1918 was 57: of whom 29 were killed and 28 died from disease. [45]

Adaptation of Ambulance Plane from Ellington 1918

Not all forced landings ended tragically, however. Cadet Ira B. McNair wrote about the experiences of another flying team in his formation one day. McNair recorded that the other pilot's plane sprang a leak in his oil tank and ran out of oil, so the airplane had to make an emergency landing about ten miles from the field at Ellington. The pilot picked out a house and landed "nice and pretty" in a field near it. They had hardly unfastened their safety belts when they saw an automobile coming out for them. The farmer had seen the boys "jazzing" around and then land in his field. The farmer drove them to the house and invited them for dinner. They had a good meal and after, the farmer invited them to the cellar and drew three glasses of real, live beer from a big keg! Texas was a dry state at the time, so this was a real surprise. Cadet McNair pondered the possibility of making such a fortunate emergency landing, "Gee! First thing you know our oil tank will run dry-I ought to put a hole in it, don't you think?" [46]

Creative Landings, from Ellington 1918

Fliers were superstitious about having their first wrecks, and there was a special designation for those who wrecked several times. Cadet Gutterson wrote:

> Saturday was the first...time I ever went up with any other pilot. Coming back, we saw a wreck, and we spiraled and got a good look at it.... I knew my pilot had got his first spill. He came out O.K. and took up another ship and he feels relieved, for until you've had your first spill you 'have it coming' and worry about it.... I saw a great smash up this morning. When a fellow smashes five ships he's a 'ca-

> det ace'. Well, I guess some fellow must have gotten a sudden desire to become an ace, because he smashed up three ships before he smashed up himself. They weren't much hurt. The fellow in the back seat was out before the ship turned over, and the pilot wasn't much behind him. He looked mighty sheepish when he crawled out through the broken struts and canvas...[47]

Pilot mortality was also high because there were no parachutes, no safety equipment, and no way to get out of a plane that was on fire and falling out of the sky. The lightweight framework of the cockpit provided little protection from impact, and the pilot's bodies were completely unprotected from engine fire and debris. Pilots in trouble simply had to ride their aircraft to the ground. Standard equipment for the flight surgeon to carry with him in the ambulance included a big two-edged ax and four-foot wire cutters to free the fliers from the wreckage in a hurry.[48] Badly wrecked airplanes were often stripped of their reusable parts then burned where they crashed to prevent the sight of the mangled planes from disheartening the other flyers.[49]

Flyers were also in danger of simply falling out of the open cockpits of the aircraft. Granville Gutterson arrived at Ellington Field in February of 1918 after graduating from ground school in Austin, Texas. In a letter dated March, 1918, just one short month after his arrival, Gutterson wrote that he was having the time of his life flying twice a day. He reported truthfully that he was never scared, although he had seen nine fatal accidents since he arrived. His description of his first flight must have scared his family though, as he wrote home:

> On my first trip the pilot tried to scare me out by making some pretty stiff banks, but it's great stuff to look down between the wings and see the ground directly underneath. Then he tried some zooms (a short dive and then a rise until you lose speed and are about to start a tail-slide, not a tailspin, and then you nose out again). I turned around and laughed at him, so he climbed up a ways and shut off the engine and did a spiral down. He shut the engine off so I could hear him and said 'Engines dead!'...But forewarned is forearmed, so I said, 'Nuts! Let her ride!' It was a great ride."[50]

His enthusiasm was still running high a month later when he wrote home about his Aerial Gunnery School at San Leon, Texas. In this training, two airplanes were assigned to a specific quadrant of airspace, where they flew to a certain altitude and maneuvered against each other, in and out of clouds, each one trying to sneak up on the other. Kodak cameras that operated like machine guns were built into the planes, except they shot photographs instead of live ammunition. These photos were developed, and the next day the gunners and pilots could take a look at their "shots," see which ship scored the most hits, and determine what corrections their aerial gunnery work needed.

Wreck taken from Ellington 1918

Cadet Gutterson's mother must have been terrified to read; "This fighting in the air is fine stuff! The only part I don't care for is that I have to unstrap to work the Kodak right, and with my pilot pulling stunts to keep the other ship from getting a shot at us, it keeps me busy staying in the ship. I fasten my straps to my legs, between my knees and ankles, so that if I should fall out I would be held until I could climb back in."[51]

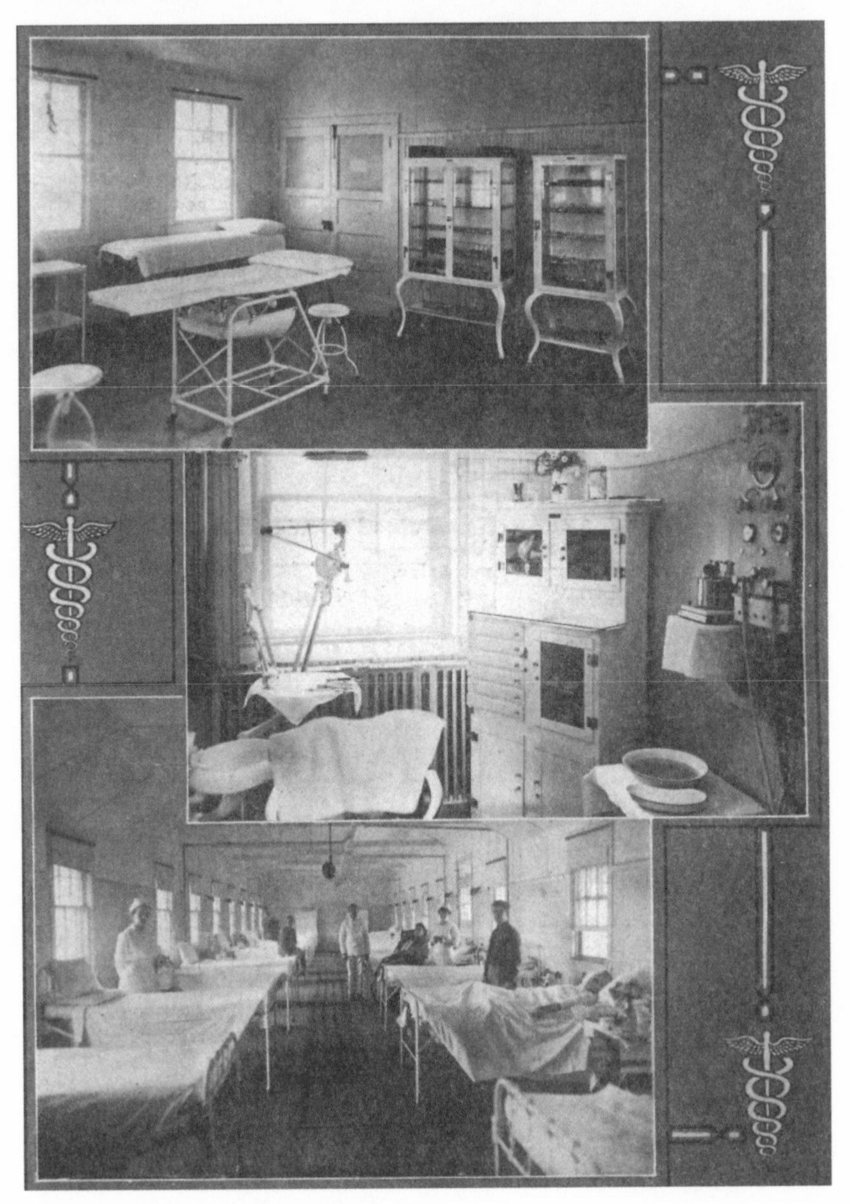

Post Hospital Interior, from Ellington 1918

The post hospital paid careful attention to the health of the fliers. The surgeons at the post hospital developed new techniques and procedures for treating the types of injuries caused by plane crashes and for dealing with the unique mental trauma aviators experienced from long falls. Ellington Field was one of the first bases to have a flight surgeon. The hospital staff also provided routine medical and dental care for the military families, inspected the barracks, mess halls and food on a regular basis, and oversaw the sanitation of the base. Overall, the men and their families probably had better, cleaner food and more frequent health care than the population at large.[52]

The Post Hospital taken from Ellington 1918

After all the hard work and hurry, by the time the United States had trained enough pilots and built enough airplanes, the air war in Europe was almost over. In the early spring of 1918, twenty members of the Twelfth Aerial Squadron from Ellington Field landed in England, one of the few crews from Ellington that had the chance to participate in the War.

Second Provisional Wing

The timing of the end of World War I changed the fate of the newly-founded Second Provisional Wing, as well. On June 5, 1918 Major Seth W. Cook was ordered to Ellington Field, Texas, to organize the Second Provisional Wing of the Army Air Corps on June 5, 1918[53]. Ellington Field was only meant to be a temporary home for the Wing, and one of the first orders of business for Major Cook was to choose a permanent location. The Army was considering two sites; one field a short distance from

Galveston, the second one at Pine Gully, east of what became the cities of Seabrook and Kemah. Ultimately, the second site was chosen, due to its closer proximity to Houston and Ellington Field, its existing water and rail facilities and general accessibility.[54]

The developers called the 258 acre site Park Place[55] , but the original official name chosen for the new field was Ream Field, in memory of Major William R. Ream, the first flying surgeon of the Army Air Service. The name was used for only two months until Army headquarters in Washington, D.C. discovered that another field in California had been already been given that name. Thereafter, until it closed, the field was simply known as Park Place.[56]

The Second Provisional Wing was primarily supported by the 190th and 191st Aero Squadrons stationed at Ellington, and later, the 343rd Aero Squadron. The Wing officers and men were housed at Ellington Field while the new site was being surveyed and sewer lines, water lines, lighting and roads were being planned and built. Ellington's hangars were used to house the first twenty airplanes and a fleet of motor trucks assigned to the Wing.

The entire Wing was ordered to Mineola, Long Island on November 13, 1918, presumably to depart from there for duty overseas. The men must have felt a great sense of purpose as the camp was emptied and the men, tents, airplanes and trucks were loaded onto the baggage cars of a train headed for the East coast. A sixty-man guard detachment of the 817th Depot Aero Squadron was sent to guard the army property left on site at Park Place. The Armistice of November 11, 1918 caused the orders for troop movement to be cancelled, and the men sadly returned to Park Place, a mere three hours after their departure. The Wing had not traveled any farther than Harrisburg, Texas, before they returned. The disbanding of the camp was begun in mid-December, 1918, and the Park Place site was soon returned to its peace-time status.[57]

Change of Command

On November 11, 1918, Ellington said goodbye to one commander and welcomed another. The base put on its finest aviation display, with two miles of airplanes stretched out across the field. Ellington's men and their families joined in the parades and celebration in Houston. The November 15th edition of the post newspaper *Tale Spins* carried a story of the celebration of the war's end: "Every officer and enlisted man on the post who could get away, it seemed, tried to crowd into the many jitneys and 6 o'clock and 7 o'clock interurban cars. Trucks were loaded to the limit and still could not accommodate the crowds going to Aviation Station and many had to walk that far. The peace celebration in town was the main attraction."[58] As the first World War ended, so did the high-flying glory years at Ellington Field. The nation took a collective sigh of relief, and ushered in the Roaring Twenties.[59]

After armistice, as the need for the airplanes, pilots, and military equipment dwindled to almost nothing, the production at the war factories ground to a halt. The women who had been so necessary in the factory and in the air service were replaced by men who came home expecting jobs. Many of the young men went back to their civilian jobs, women became homemakers again and America returned to its pre-war pursuits. The War Department closed many military bases and sold the land as surplus property. In November of 1920, most of the remaining soldiers were shipped off to another base in Michigan, and Ellington was left with a clean up and disposal crew. Ellington experienced a series of closings and partial re-openings over the next few years.

After the War was Over…

The United States Government had a surplus of planes. Bidding for the 1200 airplanes sitting unassembled in crates on the docks of the municipal wharf in Houston, Texas, was opened to the public on February 1, 1919. "The government will sell in any quantity, from 1 to 1,000. The big idea is to sell them, and if anyone wants to organize the Amalgamated Order of High Flyers, and equip its members with machines for high flying, Uncle Sam is willing."[60] An inquiry came from the King Ranch, in Kingsville, Texas. They wanted eight or ten airplanes to keep track of the great herds of cattle that wondered over the ranch's more than 800,000 acres of pastures. Train loads of unassembled aircraft were shipped to Houston's Ellington Field, which served as a depot for disposing of surplus property. Aspiring barnstormers, crop dusters and adventurers bought crated Curtis JN-1 Jennies and assembled them on the deserted runways at Ellington. Many then taught themselves how to fly.[61] Lt. Melvin Asp (1893-1964) was put in charge of disposing of the surplus at

Ellington.[62] Melvin Asp was destined to be part of military aviation. He was plummeting through the air even before there were airplanes being used in military service. As a Sergeant in Company 1, First Minnesota Infantry, he made a double parachute jump from the only hot air balloon to be used in the Mexican Border War in 1916.[63] He was assigned to Kelly Field, Texas for flight training in 1918, and remained there as an instructor until 1919. He was stationed at Ellington by January, 1920, and served there until 1923. He and his wife, Gladys, are listed on the Houston, Harris County census for 1920, along with all the other men and their families who were still at Ellington Field. [64]

Lt. Asp's time at Ellington must have been an extraordinary adventure for a man who loved to fly. He had all those crates of airplanes, stacks of parts, and the mostly unused hangars, runways, and maintenance shops to play in. He built several airplanes that were smaller and faster than anything else in the air while he was at Ellington. On August 13, 1922, he won the air Southern Aerial Derby in a diminutive airplane he built called the "Skeeter."[65] The Skeeter was powered by a three cylinder motor and had remarkable climbing power. It was capable of climbing 20,000 feet in 20 minutes[66] and flew at more than 150 miles an hour.[67] Lt. Asp and Capt. Aubrey I. Engle, who was also stationed at Ellington, built another airplane nicknamed the "Aerial Ant." The upper wingspan of the "Ant" was eighteen feet, while the lower wing span was only fourteen feet-four feet shorter. The new plane was driven by a 60 horsepower Lawrence Sperry motor and had already demonstrated an airspeed of 145 miles an hour, which was one-third faster than the "Messenger" scout airplane the Army Air Service had boasted was the fastest plane in the air. The "Ant" was fast, strong, and maneuverable. On a test flight at Ellington, Lt. Asp took off in less than fifty feet, attained an altitude of 1,000 feet in thirty seconds, and outflew a D-H and an SE-5. [68] A few days after the Southern Aerial Derby success, *The Houston Post* newspaper proudly announced that Lt. Melvin Asp's entry into the big Pulitzer Trophy Race at Selfridge Field near Detroit, Michigan had been accepted. Houston and Ellington Field would be represented among the best flyers of the time, including Wiley Post, Jimmy Doolittle and Frank Hawks, among other pioneers of aviation. Lt. Asp finished his job and left Ellington Field in 1923.

In 1921, the First Pursuit Group, commanded by Major, later General, Carl Spaatz, occupied the airfield for one year. Ellington then closed for a while and opened again from 1923 to 1926 as a base for the air services division of the recently reorganized 36th Division of the Texas National Guard.[69] The 36th Division used the field as a training base from September of 1923 until January of 1927. The squadron moved to the Houston Municipal Air Field after a fire razed the remaining buildings at Ellington. The War Department had begun dismantling parts of the base as early as 1925, and by the end of 1926, closed down the famous little airfield that had once been promoted by Houston politicians as the national hub of the air age, and sold all its equipment for $14,700.[70]

The following story perfectly illustrated how complete Ellington's fall from glory was. In 1925, two Army Air Service Douglas World Cruisers and their crews flew around the world in a record five months and 22 days. On their celebratory tour across the country, they stopped at historic Ellington Field to allow the public to view the airplanes and ask questions. The once-bustling military city was now only a deserted field and there was little evidence that it had ever been one of the world's "premier training schools for aviators." The only thing left of mighty Ellington Field was the runway. Despite the arrival of the famous world-hopping crew and their airplanes, there was no local turnout to see the famous flyers, because Ellington Field, now only a cow pasture, was under quarantine due to an outbreak of hoof and mouth disease among the cattle that grazed near the runway, and that caused more excitement than the airplanes.[71]

By 1930, even the underground water pipes and the railroad siding had been removed. From 1930 to 1940, the open land was leased for grazing.[72] Ellington Field had come full circle and was once again a place where cows could graze peacefully, unmolested by errant bombers and noisy airplane engines.

Postscript About the Book, *Ellington 1918*

Armistice brought many changes, and one which made this book and all the books and articles written about the early days of Ellington Field possible was the end of war-time censorship. Before the end of the war, no written material was sent anywhere in this country without being looked over for possible breaches of information useful to the enemy, and even personal letters often had lines blacked out. Photographs of airplanes, airplane wrecks, and base buildings and personnel, which are abundant in the book, were absolutely forbidden. War shortages of material delayed the printing and manufacturing of the books. The cockpits of the De Haviland planes were ravaged for their upholstery, which gave the books their dressy brown covers. A set of R.M.A wings and the title, *Ellington, 1918*, was stamped on the covers in silver. The day-to-day military lives of the flyers, mechanics, gunners, bombardiers, navigators, instructors and other personnel at the field were laid out in simple, humorous stories, with plenty of cartoons and photographs illustrating the text.

On Saturday, February 1, 1919, the publication of the book *Ellington 1918* was celebrated with lots of fanfare and flash. The Ellington Field Band played, movie reels made by the field photographer and soldiers stationed at the base were shown, and there was a lantern slide show. Lt. C.W. Wright and Lt. Joe Weil, members of the editorial staff, "bombed" Galevston Island with advertising flyers about the book on March 4.[73] The staff of men who put the book together had reason to be proud; it was the first story of war flying in America written by men who were stationed at the premier flying training field in the country.[74] Fathers and mothers could finally read about what their boys had been doing all that time in faraway Texas. It was also the first time the public had a chance to see the photographs, wrecks and all. The men who served at Ellington had a written and visual record they could treasure for years.

"What did you do in the war, dear? I served at Ellington Field!"

Commercial Ads from Ellington 1918

SAN LEON

"The Bright Spot of Texas"

BAYSHORE BUILDING SITES AND FARM HOME TRACTS AT POPULAR PRICES

Beautiful Bayshore Building Sites, overlooking the sparkling waters of Trinity and Galveston Bays, may be bought at San Leon at $50 to $75 per lot.

San Leon is situated on the bayshore, almost midway between Houston and Galveston. Two shelled roads connect it with about 500 miles of other hard-surfaced roads, thus making it the automobilists' paradise.

Bathing, boating and fishing cannot be excelled at San Leon. Wild ducks flock to the waters near San Leon by the thousands. Extra large and deliciously flavored oysters in almost unlimited quantities are gathered within a few steps of the beach at San Leon. Red Fish Reef, just opposite San Leon, is noted for its fine fishing.

San Leon is delightfully cool in summer, being almost constantly fanned by the breeze right off of the Gulf of Mexico, and it is very mild in winter.

A few improved and unimproved farm homesites, from five acres up, contiguous to San Leon, can be bought at reasonable prices. Between 300 and 400 acres of the San Leon Farm Home tracts were under cultivation in 1918.

San Leon As a Prospective Oil Field

San Leon is within sight of the famous Goose Creek oil field. Geologists and oil men predict an oil field underlies the property. A test well in search of oil will be drilled on the San Leon townsite, commencing in the early spring of 1919.

With each lot sold, we give a $30 interest in the proposed oil company. All oil rights under the lots we sell goes to the purchaser.

Write for our prospectus containing a hundred or more views of San Leon and the surrounding territory, a bird's-eye view of the Houston-Galveston district, showing 500 miles or more of hard-surfaced roads in the district, the various oil fields, etc., as well as the written opinion of two geologists and oil men as to the possibilities of developing an oil field at San Leon.

SAN LEON COMPANY

212-213 BEATTY BUILDING——HOUSTON, TEXAS

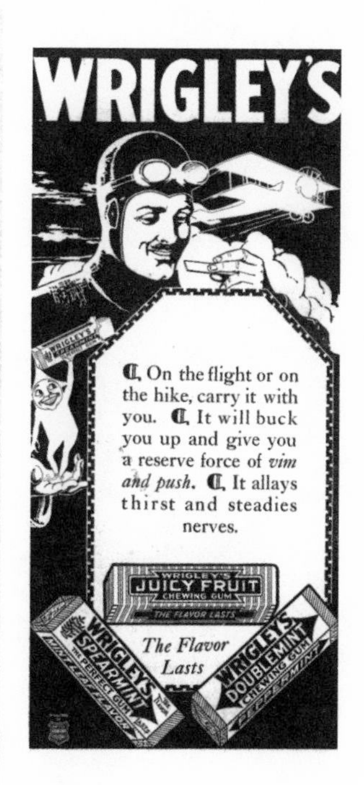

Lest We Forget...

KILLED

Adams, Chester A., 2nd Lt., Abilene, TX, Nov. 18, 1918
Belser, King, 2nd Lt., Snyder AR, Oct. 4, 1918
Bradley, Wayles B., Cadet, Baltimore, MD, Feb. 4, 1918
Bremer, Clarence J, Cadet, Paxton, IL, Mar. 2, 1918
Carroll, Gerald V., Cadet, Passaic NJ, Jan. 16, 1918
Cole, Charles C., 2nd Lt., Dec. 6, 1918
Compton, James H., Pvt. Texarkana, TX Mar. 2, 1918
Cone, Edmund L., 2nd Lt. New York City, NY June 28, 1918
Davis, Louis E., 2nd Lt. Bloomington, IL, May 10, 1918
Dixon, Jerome J., 2nd Lt., Brooklyn, NY, Dec. 9, 1918
Dwiggins, Russell H., 2nd Lt., Waynetown, IN, Apr. 4, 1918
Earle, Marion M., 2nd Lt., Lewisburg, PA Mar. 14, 1918
Earner, John J., Pvt. June 4, 1918
Eckstrand, Carl E., Cadet, Apr. 4, 1918
Elliott, Hammitt K., 2nd Lt., Feb. 27, 1918
Gelwick, Miles W., 2nd Lt., Findlay, OH, Mar. 14, 1918
Gleason, Donald W., Cadet, Delhi, NY, Feb. 14, 1918
Ives, Joseph F., Cadet, Chicago, IL, Apr. 4, 1918
James, Edwin D., 2nd Lt., Toledo, OH, Jan. 30, 1918
Jones, Forrest E., Cadet, Apr. 16, 1918
Mather, Carl S., Cadet, Paw Paw MI, Jan. 30, 1918
Maurice, Benjamin E., 2nd Lt., Mamaroneck, NY, May 13, 1918
Maxwell, Morris F., 2nd Lt., New Hope, PA, Oct 30, 1918
McGranahan, Joseph F., 2nd Lt., Jamestown, PA, Nov. 7, 1918
Montgomery, Roger, 1st Lt., Tunica, MS, June 11, 1918
Nugent, Leo J., 2nd Lt., Cedar Falls, IA, Apr. 16, 1918
Probst, Earl R., Pvt., June 15, 1918
Stephenson, James T. Chfr, Houston, TX, Dec. 4, 1918
Winterton, Roland J, 2nd Lt., Apr. 16, 1918

DIED OF DISEASE

Baker, Herbert L. Pvt., Brockton, MA, Dec. 9, 1918
Benjamin, Everett F., 2nd Lt., Riverhead, L.I., Oct. 12, 1918
Bergh, James R., 2nd Lt., Eau Claire, WI, Nov. 1, 1918
Beyler, George H., Pvt., Madison, WI, Sep. 4, 1918
Brigham, John I., Pvt., Youngstown, OH, Oct. 18, 1918

Cameron, Michael G., Pvt., Hampton, MA, Dec. 10, 1918
Cobb, Henry E., Cadet, Seymour, IN, April 23, 1918
Courtney, Rance, Pvt., Denver, CO, Feb. 25, 1918
Domke, Rudolph I., M.S.E., Chicago, IL, Dec. 9, 1918
Fleming, Jack B., Pvt., Childress, TX, Oct. 28, 1918
Greer, Don W., Pvt., League City, TX, Oct. 24, 1918
Gutterson, Granville, 2nd Lt., St. Paul, MN Dec. 4, 1918
Hepler, Howard, Pvt., South Bend, IN, Oct. 5, 1918
Holmberg, Gustave A., 2nd Lt., Rockford, IL, Oct. 18, 1918
Leithold, Frederick, Pvt., Philadelphia, PA, Oct. 15, 1918
May, Worthington H., Pvt., Brooklyn, NY, Feb. 16, 1918
McGuire, James, Chfr, New York City, NY, Nov. 26, 1918
Plankenhorn, James E., Cpl., Montoursville, PA, Oct. 13, 1918
Read, James K. 2nd Lt., Chicago, IL, Oct. 9, 1918
Roberts, Guy, Pvt., Crystal City, MO, Oct. 8, 1918
Sharon, Edward C., Pvt., Haggerston, MD, Oct. 15, 1918
Shipp. Ernest, Sgt., Timpson, TX, Feb. 12, 1918
Stafford, Edward, Pvt. Belleville, TX, Feb. 8, 1918
Statham. Gordon L., 2nd Lt., Americus, GA, May 2, 1918
Taylor, William P., Cadet, Salisbury, MD., Oct. 19, 1918
Turner, William R. Pvt., Houston, TX Oct. 20, 1918
Willett, Charles W., Pvt., Argo, AL, Aug. 22, 1918
Wiser, George E., Toledo, OH, Oct. 21, 1918

Funeral Cortege Courtesy Marlene Champion Collection

End Notes

[1] Roger Bilstein and Jay Miller, *Aviation in Texas* (San Antonio: Texas Monthly Press, 1985), 51.

[2] *History of Ellington Field,* Houston Airport System, www.ci.Houston.tx.us/has.

[3] Dr. Kent McLemore, Assistant, Deputy Director for Planning, Houston Airport System. Interview by author, notes, March 12, 2003, Houston, Texas.

[4] Erik Carlson, *Ellington Field: A Short History, 1917-1963* (Houston: NASA, 1999), 8.

[5] Ibid., 9.

[6] Jim Higgins, *Ellington Field, 1917. Houston Chronicle*, Texas Section, Nov. 1, 1987, 5.

[7] See Biography Section.

[8] Department of the Air Force, Office of Information Services, *A Chronology of American Aerospace Events* (Washington, 1959), 2 states the Aeronautical Division... under Capt. Charles DeF. Chandler, was to have charge of "all matters pertaining to military ballooning, air machines and kindred subjects."

[9] Ibid., 18.

[10] Marguerite Johnston, *Houston, the Unknown City, 1836-1946* (College Station: Texas A&M University Press, fourth printing, 1994), 207,208.

[11] USAF History Museum, WWI Production, www.wpafb.af.mil/museum/history/ww1/ww1-1a.htm. Accessed 12/2/2001.

[12] A Chronology of American Aerospace Events, Department of the Air Force, Office of Information Services (Washington, 1959), 17.

[13] Ibid.

[14] Lt. Joe Stack, in *Ellington 1918.* (Houston: Private printing, 1918), 29.

[15] "Signal Corps No. 1, Purchasing and Supporting the Army's First Airplane," www.airforcehistory.hq.af.mil/soi/signal.htm, 3.

[16] Stack, 3.

[17] Ibid.

[18] Capt. Cyrus C. Smythe made the first flight, Stack, p.5

[19] George E.A. Hallett, *Airplane Motors; A Course of Practical Instruction in Their Care and Overhauling for the Use of Military Aviators,* (Washington, Government Printing Office, 1917), 5.

[20] "Ellington Was Tents on Mud In '17, Cadet Then Recalls Here", *The Houston Post,* March 7, 1941.

[21] Ira B. McNair, letters to family, October 1 to December 23, 1918. Copies in possession of author.

[22] "The First Round-The-World Flight", www.wpafb.af.mil/museum/history/.

[23] *Space News Roundup*, August 3, 1984. Vol. 23, No. 14. JSC History Collection, 3.

[24] U.S. Signal Corps Agreement and Specifications for a Heavier-Than-Air Flying Machine, Specification No. 286, General Requirements Section, Paragraph 4. See Appendix 6 for complete copy of the Information Packet sent out from the U.S. Army Signal Corps to the Wright Brothers. Part of the specifications required that any plane delivered be guaranteed to fly forty miles an hour.

[25] See Biography section.
[26] Gilbert Gutterson, *Granville, Tales and Tailspins From A Flyer's Diary*. (New York: Abingdon Press, 1919), 20-23.
[27] Stack, 81.
[28] Ibid.
[29] Lt. Lars LaRue, in *Ellington 1918* (Houston: Private printing, 1918), 49.
[30] Photo of Aerial Gunner at San Leon.
[31] Gutterson, 31-33.
[32] Ibid., 85.
[33] California Death Index, 1940-1997, indicated birth date of 22 March, 1882, birthplace "Other Country", death date 27 January, 1956, death place Santa Barbara County, California, and mother's maiden name as Muir.
[34] Stack, 8.
[35] Ibid., 7.
[36] Ibid., 81.
[37] Ibid.
[38] Major Robert B. Hunter, in *Ellington 1918,* 33.
[39] Stack, 7.
[40] Lt. Garrett Graham, in *Ellington, 1918,* 11.
[41] Ibid.
[42] Ibid., 13.
[43] Bilstein and Miller, 52.
[44] *Houston Chronicle,* January 1, 1918, January 2, 1918.
[45] Ibid., January 17.
[46] *In Memoriam*, Maj. Robert J. Hunter, *Ellington 1918,* 97. (*Note*: list did not include Sgt. Sam Norvick, killed Dec. 31, 1917.)
[47] McNair letters, October 1, 1918.
[48] Gutterson, 19, 20.
[49] Gutterson, 20.
[50] Graham, 11.
[51] Gutterson, 14-16.
[52] Gutterson, 19.
[53] Graham, 37.
[54] *Overseas Dreams: Second Provisional Wing,* Bertram H. Yarwood, ed. (Houston: Gulfport Printing Company, 1919), pp. 21, 22.
[55] Ibid., p. 22.
[56] Ibid., p. 2.
[57] Ibid., p. 25.
[58] Ibid., pp. 25, 26.
[59] As reproduced in *Space News Roundup*, August 3, 1984. Vol. 23, No. 14. JSC Historical Collection, 3.
[60] Johnston, 207, 208.
[61] *Houston Chronicle*, January 15, 1919.
[62] *Houston's Aviation History Timeline,* The 1940 Air Terminal Museum website, at www.1940airterminal.org.

[63] *The Houston Post,* August 17, 1922.

[64] Newspaper article, no citation, courtesy of Dennis Cole, 4 April, 2007.

[65] 1920 Census, Harris County, Texas, 262. The census for Ellington Field is six pages and lists seventy men, thirty four family members, two nurses, and thirty six Chinese laborers. There may have been others who lived off base, but as off base housing was very limited, this census listing probably reflect the majority of men still at Ellington.

[66] *Houston Chronicle,* August 14, 1922.

[67] Ibid.

[68] *Houston Chronicle,* August 6, 1922.

[69] *The Houston Post,* August 17, 1922.

[70] "Post War Period", Texas Military Forces Museum website at www.kwanah.com/txmilmus/tnghist, 2.

[71] Johnston, 256.

[72] *Space News Roundup*, August 3, 1984. Vol. 23, No. 14. JSC Historical Collection, 4.

[73] *Houston Chronicle*. June 6, 1940.

[74] *Houston Chronicle,* March 4, 1919.

[75] *Houston Chronicle,* February 2, 1919.

CHAPTER II

World War II, 1941-1945, Ellington Field Reopens

Lt. Havins, Ellington Field Historical Officer: *When was the decision reached to reopen Ellington Field?*

Col. Reid, Ellington Field Commander: *The decision was reached in April, 1940. It was in the minds of those who made the decision to establish the field and provide four-way training. At first it was expected that there would be pilot, advanced navigator, bombardment, and gunnery training.*

Lt. Havins: *I noted a memorandum in the files containing the names of certain officers who were scheduled to come to this post. Did Randolph (Field) officials choose them?*

Col. Reid: *"No, I chose them."*

Interview with Colonel Walter H. Reid, Base Commander, by Historical Officer, Lt. T. R. Havins, 28 October 1943.[1]

By 1940, as World War II loomed on the horizon, aviation technology had made tremendous strides all over the world. America no longer just sent its soldiers "off to war;" war was now capable of coming to America, by sea and air. As the United States government became aware of the vulnerability of the entire country to air attack and of its coastlines to an attack by submarines, new defensive strategies were put in place across the nation. The War Department reactivated idle military bases and built new ones. Congress appropriated $7 million dollars to rebuild Ellington Field.[2] The government also purchased the northern two-thirds of Matagorda Island, off the coast of Texas, to use as a bombing range for crews who would be trained at Ellington Field and other bases in Texas.[3]

As early as 1934, the Houston Chamber of Commerce had prepared an extensive brief pointing out the strategic proximity of Houston to the concentration of the booming oil refining industry along the Houston Ship Channel and the gulf coast. This brief asked for a tactical air force to be located at Ellington Field as a protective measure. In 1940, the Chamber renewed its efforts when it appeared certain the United States was going to become involved in World War II.[4] Houston newspapers followed the attempted resurrection of the old airfield:

> Two important factors had much to do with the establishment of the United States Air Corps Bombardment Academy at Ellington Field, near Houston. One of these was the close proximity of adequate bombing ranges along the Texas coast. The other was the existence in South Texas of an expanding industry that might need immediate and competent protection.... In September, 1940, the Quartermaster Corps of the Army was ordered to initiate necessary work to launch the building of one of the largest Air Corps Reservations in the United States. Approximately 1600 acres of land, spotted with a few landmarks of the old Ellington, was to be reclaimed and on it constructed another link in the vast program of national defense. Approximately 300 men were put to work immediately, preparing for the construction gangs at Ellington Field. The work was well on its way when the Engineering Corps took over in December to speed events.[5]

On November 23, 1940, Ellington was designated as an Air Corps station under the temporary command of Capt. H.L. Borden.[6] The base officially opened Dec. 1, 1940, with Lt. Col. Walter H. Reid as Commanding Officer. (See biography section) This was Col Reid's fourth tour of duty at Ellington. He was first transferred to Ellington Field as a Lieutenant in March, 1918, to finish his Army Air Corps training, again from 1920-1922 with the First Pursuit Group, and then from 1926-1931 with the

111th Observation Squadron.[7] Col. Reid had been an active part of much of Ellington's history, and was keenly interested in preserving at least some of its heritage. He arranged for internationally recognized Houston painter Emma Richardson Cherry (his mother-in-law) to paint a portrait of Lt. Eric Lamar Ellington. "to be prominently displayed in the field headquarters as an enduring symbol of the historic linkage between the earlier World War I airfield and the new one that was now poised on the threshold of yet another international conflict."[8]

The Army Corps of Engineers arrived to speed up the construction of the new air field in December of 1940, which allowed the work to proceed twenty-four hours a day. The number of construction employees jumped from about 300 to 1500, and buildings began to appear rapidly. The first problems the crews tackled were water supply, drainage and adequate sewage systems, so that the new aviation cadets would not have to live in rows of tents in the mud, as their predecessors did in 1917. Barracks appeared in neat rows. Five mess halls accommodated the hungry soldiers, along with warehouses, office buildings and a field hospital. The construction of all 165 frame buildings on Ellington was completed by April 1, 1941. The new warehouses filled with the equipment and supplies needed to run an army post with a population of 4,200 officers and men. Telecommunications specialists laid more than 140 miles of wire to facilitate the radio communication, control systems, beam systems and telephone service required. [9]

New Barracks at Ellington, Courtesy of Ellington Field Historian's Office

Of special interest to local reporters was the installation of a highly secret type of equipment rumored to be effective at detecting oncoming enemy airplanes. "This equipment," said Assistant Chief of Staff General George V. Strong, to the Senate Committee, "the design of which is of a highly secret nature, apparently is far advanced of any similar equipment available to any of the belligerents abroad.... In the light of present world conditions, further delay in providing means to afford a reasonable defense against a known possible hostile nation appears inexcusable." [10] The mysterious equipment that had been installed under such secrecy at Ellington was the latest version of radar. Radar was the newest technology for the detection and early warning of an attack from the air or from the sea.

The new airplanes had to be housed better than the World War I era JN-4's, so engineers built two huge steel-reinforced hangars that covered 42,000 square feet of ground. Because of the enormous expense, the Corps of Engineers ultimately decided to build only enough hangar space to house aircraft in need of service or repair, with additional tie-down space on the concrete aprons of the runways for all other aircraft. The new aircraft were too heavy to take off from the old packed mud and gravel runways, so new runways had to be built.

The Corps of Engineers called in contractors from all over the United States to assist in the massive concrete work. The Tellepsen Construction Company of Houston oversaw the designing and pouring of one of the largest single pieces of concrete in the world. By the end of the project, the runway slab alone covered 545,000 square feet of ground. Construction Chief Major Homer G. Olmstead remarked, "All in all, something like 200 miles of 20-foot highway could have been laid with the concrete poured at Ellington Field."[11] The field was now ready for the road builders and heavy tractors moved in to finish the three main roads, smaller cross streets, parking lots, and two big entrances off the Galveston Highway.

Five aircraft control towers located up and down the runways directed landings and takeoffs. Each tower was equipped with two-way communication, and each had full jurisdiction over a specified area of the landing field.[12] On the 26th of June 1941, base commander Lt. Col. Walter H. Reid ceremonally landed the first plane on the concrete runway at the newly rebuilt Ellington Field, and the airfield was declared officially ready for use.

On Oct. 6, 1941, the first fifty aviation students began their advanced pilot training at Ellington Field.[13] The cadets were young men between the ages of twenty-one and twenty-seven, and most were college graduates. These young recruits listed their prior civilian jobs on their induction papers as: newspaperman, salesman, accountant, chemist, surveyor, engineer, welder, spark-plug inspector, bricklayers' helper, seaman, cattleman, farmer, musician, actor, riding instructor, and student. Monday through Friday, their days began with reveille at 5:15 A.M. and then breakfast at 5:55 A.M. The students attended ground school classes from 7:30 A.M. to 10:00A.M. followed by athletics, then lunch at 11:25 A.M. Their afternoon was taken up with flying instruction from 12:30 P.M. until 5:35 P.M. A call to quarters came at 10:30 P.M., and Taps sounded at 11:00 P.M. On Saturday the men had an inspection at 8:00A.M. and drill from 8:30 A.M. to 11:00 A.M., after which they were free until Monday morning.[14]

Instruction in flying began on the first day, and the first few weeks were filled with Instrument Flying, Formation Flying, and Altitude Flying. By the fourth week, the students had completed coursework in both Day and Night Navigation and Night Flying. By the end of the ten-week course, each aviator-in-training had charted a minimum of seventy hours of flight time in his personal Pilot Log Book.

The flying training also included about fifteen hours of practice in a device called the Link trainer. The Link trainer was a flight-simulator commonly referred to as "The Blue Box" because it was a large box-shaped chamber the student entered that contained a complete replica of a cockpit, with full instrumentation. The box was mounted on a system of hydraulic jacks that allowed it to mimic the movement of a real airplane in response to the student's manipulation of the cockpit instruments. Time spent in the Link trainer was the cause of much frustration to the students. Referring to the constant grumbling directed at the training device, one Cadet Dyar wrote in a column in the post newspaper, *Tailspin:* "Though why we should cuss, I don't know…it's the only place where you can crash fatally three times in a half-hour and still be able to get out and light a cigarette afterward…if you can get the match to quit shaking."[15] The students logged an average of fifteen hours in the Link trainer, most of it in the first half of the course.

This first class of student aviators faced a situation more hazardous than any of the classes that followed because the new ground crews were not yet familiar with how the field operated. Crowded conditions on the runway access ramps, inexperienced maintenance personnel, and novice control tower operators made the coordination of the flights taking off and landing on the runways difficult. In addition, boxes of airplane parts and military gear arrived daily and further crowded the runways and hangars. The unsettled conditions at the new field favored accidents. Major J. W. Andrew, in a letter to all students, urged the use of good judgment, and pointed out that the slightest lapse of attention could result in fatalities. These first fifty students must have listened, because the only accidents recorded at the end of the course were two "ground loops," the euphemism used when novice pilots ran off the runway and got the airplanes stuck in the mud.[16]

Parachutists from Astro-Dome Advanced Navigators Class of 1944 Yearbook

One of the students trained at Ellington Field during this time later became the nation's most famous test pilot. On September 12, 1941, Charles E. "Chuck" Yeager enlisted as a private in the Army Air Corps, and completed his basic training at Ellington Field. That early training was a far cry from the flight he took in the Bell-X-1 aircraft on October 14, 1947 at Edwards Air Force Base in California, when he became the first man to fly faster than the speed of sound.[17]

Ellington Field had been the top training school for bombardiers in World War I, and in 1941, newspaper articles proudly announced that Ellington Field would once again become the "Bombardment Academy of the Air." On October 6, 1941, thirty cadets and Capt. E. C. Plummer began a twelve-week course.[18] By the end of this course, the students had spent nine weeks in ground school, an average of eighteen hours training in the mighty twin-engine AT-17s, and had dropped about seventy practice bombs. The bombs used in practice were shells weighing twenty pounds apiece that were filled with seventy-five pounds of sand and five pounds of black powder. As in the early days, bombs dropped during the day gave off a plume of smoke so the bombardiers could tell if they were on target, and at night, a light flashed as the bombs hit the targets.

As it turned out, the first class was the only class of advanced bombardier training that was completed at Ellington. By the third week of the new program, it was apparent that the frequent rainy weather and cloudy conditions in Houston made it a less-than-ideal location for bombing training, which required visual contact with the ground from very high altitudes, much higher than during World War I. During one week, instructors had to cancel sixty-five practice runs due to impeded visibility, and the total cancelled during the entire course was about 250 runs. The War Department decided to move advanced bombardment training from Ellington Field to Midland, Texas, and Albuquerque, New Mexico. The War Department announcement cited "low ceilings and rainy weather" as the reasons for the change of location.[19]

Within a few days of the beginning of American participation in World War II, Ellington Field had graduated fifty pilots, twenty-eight bombardiers, and one hundred and forty-four preflight cadets. All fifty students in that first class survived both academically and physically and graduated on December 12, 1941, just five days after the attack on Pearl Harbor. Within a few days, the graduates were widely scattered, and some went directly to the war's front lines. The first man in this first class to be killed in action was Lt. Charles N. Chapman, Jr. In honor of his sacrifice, one of the streets at Ellington Field was named for him. Although Ellington was not destined to once again become the "Bombardment Academy of the Air," many of the pilots, advanced navigators, and aerial gunners who served in World War II trained there.

Men continued to arrive at Ellington Field as recruitment drives intensified all across the country from 1941 to 1944, The population at Ellington Field doubled and then tripled with the new recruits. At the beginning of 1942, number of people assigned at Ellington Field was 4,774, but by the end of 1942, the number of personnel was almost 13,500.[20] Sgt. Robert G. Hahn, a recruit from Pennsylvania, recalled his induction and trip to the wilds of Texas, "Our group of approximately 310 men left the New Cumberland (Pennsylvania) Reception Center on 18 July 1941.... We had been issued a small amount of clothing, given a portion of our inoculations, and trained to the extent that we knew enough to move on 'forward march', stop on 'halt', and salute anything that glistened...We traveled for three days, and arrived at Ellington Field. ...The trip was very tiresome, dirty, and extremely uneventful. We had only one khaki uniform, and wore it for about a week. This alone made our first days miserable.... "[21]

In 1941, the train was not air-conditioned, and neither were the barracks. Since these men arrived from the north in July, the heat and humidity of the Houston summer must have hit them like a hammer and could only have added to their misery. The men had one month to settle in before they experienced Houston weather at its most intense. On September 22, 1941, the Post commander ordered the evacuation of Ellington Field due to a hurricane.[22]

Medical care for the recruits on base and their families was provided at the base hospital. The Army Air Forces Pilot School activated the base hospital on March 28, 1941. The hospital complex consisted of thirteen buildings and a staff of nine officers and fourteen enlisted men.[23] The medical personnel faced two big problems that first year of operation: sanitation and lack of trained personnel. Sanitation was a problem on the newly-built base because the copious amounts of rain that fell on the unpaved roads and bare earth caused the base to become a sea of mud and created a definite mosquito problem. Military personnel referred to the base as "Lake Ellington."[24] Recruiting and keeping enough medical personnel, especially doctors and surgeons, was always a problem. The medical staff at Ellington began a training program and by the end of 1941, all of the enlisted men of the Medical Detachment had earned Red Cross First Aid Certificates.[25]

The base hospital furnished hospitalization, medical and dental services, as well as sanitary inspections of the base environment and food supplies. By 1943, wartime expansion of the base put a strain on the basic facilities and increased the load of patients at the hospital. As of December 31, 1941, ninety-four patients had been admitted to the hospital. During the year 1942, 4,124 patients were admitted.[26] In 1943, base doctors treated 1,982 cases of various illnesses and performed seven hundred and eighty-seven operations. The base hospital also furnished medical services to fifteen satellite organizations in surrounding areas. Three of the satellite units, the Galveston Army Air Base, the Houston Military Police Battalion, and the Houston Induction Station, called on the hospital at Ellington for considerable aid. In the most serious medical cases, the hospital at Ellington evacuated patients to McCloskey General Hospital in Temple, Texas. During 1943, one hundred and -sixty-eight patients had injuries or illnesses serious enough to require evacuation.

One of the most active departments at the base hospital was the Flight Surgeon's unit. The Flight Surgeon's work consisted of the routine physical examination, assessment and ongoing care of the flyers. The care of the flyers took up the most time, but the Flight Surgeon Unit was also responsible for emergency response to the frequent crash calls that were inevitable at any large flight training school. A Flight Surgeon's report was required to complete all crash and accident investigations.

The hospital was as comfortable and complete as could be expected in an un-air conditioned building on a spartan military base. The hospital mess hall could accommodate about five hundred people a day. Food rationing and shortages caused difficulties in keeping the high calories necessary in the patient's food. Simple services, like finding a reliable service to pick up and return the hospital laundry every day, were not established for almost a year. Serving five hundred meals a day involved hours of preparation and clean up, most of which was done by hand, or rather, by a lot of hands. During all these difficulties, each member of the hospital staff was subject to transfer at any moment, and both the number of doctors and staff available and the level of individual training was in a constant state of flux. Consequently, military personnel were assigned tasks based on need, and many officers served in more than one capacity. The Camp Surgeon frequently doubled as the base veterinarian. Eight of the Women's Army Nurses were pulled into duty as hospital cooks. The hiring of local civilians was difficult, because every able-bodied man had been drafted into the service, leaving the local population not only depleted, but also facing the same work shortages as the military. Ellington Field was twelve miles from the nearest city of any size, and gas rationing made transportation to and from the base difficult, further narrowing the available labor pool.

HELEN A. BROWN
Second Lieutenant
Nurse

RUTH E. BRYANT
Second Lieutenant
Nurse

MARY S. CRAWFORD
Second Lieutenant
Nurse

JEWEL M. FULLER
Second Lieutenant
Nurse

MILDRED A. HELANDER
Second Lieutenant
Nurse

EVA L. JETT
Second Lieutenant
Nurse

The Camp Surgeon was also responsible for disease control. His duties in this area were as varied as monitoring the insect and rodent population to prevent cholera, inspecting the drainage for mosquito control and to prevent malaria, testing the water for bacteria and educating the post personnel regarding venereal and other communicable diseases. The Camp Surgeon appointed two venereal disease control officers, and instituted a regular program of education with films and lectures. The hospital provided vaccinations for typhoid fever, tetanus, yellow fever, typhus, cholera and smallpox.

Notes in the Camp Surgeon's Report hinted at the trial and error use of new drugs available for the treatment of disease and for anesthesia that might have occurred in the base hospital. In one note about the treatment of gonorrhea, the surgeon lamented that they had not cured 45% of the cases with the use of sulfa drugs, and noted the larger doses and confinement officially recommended by the Army produced no measurable difference in the recovery rate. In his opinion, there was no benefit to the larger doses or hospitalization, so he reduced the doses and treated the men as outpatients.[27] In another note, the point was made that during 1942 and 1943 there had been two hundred and twenty-five consecutive appendectomies performed, with no deaths resulting from the surgeries. It seemed to be a point of pride that no one had died during any of the procedures.

Wartime shortages of medical supplies and food rationing strained the base hospital's resources further. These shortages affected the availability of many of the medicines needed by the hospital. Sometimes the doctors had to try new combinations of available medicines, or use up old supplies, as indicated in the following note; "Spinal anesthesia, using a mixture of Novocain and pentocaine, were used in the majority of cases with satisfactory results. The instances of spinal anesthesia failure were reduced practically to none when fresh batches of Novocain and pentocaine were used. In one lot of Novocain crystals there was found a Blue Eagle label, denoting the age of the crystals, and it is believed that some of the spinal failures encountered previously were due to using old supplies."[28] Apparently, the medicines sent to the base included some that had been in storage since World War I.

Mother Nature routinely made the hospital staff's job infinitely harder. Besides every day cases of malaria, heat exhaustion, and rashes caused by the humid climate, occasionally hurricanes or tornadoes struck the area. On July 27, 1943, a tropical hurricane struck Ellington Field. Offshore radar had given no indication of the intensity of the storm and the base was unprepared for the storm's impact and duration. There was no time for the pilots to fly the airplanes out, so they tied the airplanes down to the concrete aprons of the runway with cables, and men used their body weight and hung onto the lines for several hours to keep the airplanes in place. Corporal Vaughan

Radcliffe was one of the men holding onto those cables for his life. He remembered "The hurricane came up without warning during the night. All the mechanics were sent out to the field to secure the planes. We held onto the lines, and the wind picked us right up off our feet. It was a long night...."[29]

Cpl. Radcliffe was not injured, but nearly 200 casualties were treated and 25 patients were admitted to the hospital. Six of those were seriously injured, but all recovered. In addition, every building on the base was damaged to some extent. Light, power, and telephone service were disrupted for several days. Because of flooding and ruptured lines, the Camp Surgeon declared the water supply on base unsafe. As a result of the base's experience with the hurricane, the Camp Surgeon had an auxiliary power unit installed in the hospital, so that in the next emergency, the base hospital could continue its vital service.[30]

Regardless of the trying circumstances of transferring personnel and wartime shortages, the welfare of the patients was always the top consideration for the hospital staff. The total population on the base at any one time probably never exceeded 7,000, but the constant transfer of new soldiers in and out and the addition of health care for the soldier's families made the burden of healthcare on the hospital staff much larger. In 1944, the hospital staff saw 18,842 military patients, 4,462 civilian patients, gave 58,494 immunizations and performed 14,312 physicals.[31]

The Red Cross

A part-time Red Cross field office was set up on base in July, 194, to assist the hospital staff. On March 7, 1942, the War Department directed that each field having more than 2,500 personnel was to have an on-site Red Cross unit, and the Red Cross assigned a full-time Field Director to Ellington. In October of 1943, the Red Cross added an Assistant Field Director at the base hospital.

The Field Director and his assistant served as medical social workers whose main function was to help the soldiers and their families solve their personal problems. Military life was an adventure for many young married couples, but for others the stress of moving, finding housing, and living the military life was difficult. The counseling service offered by the Red Cross eased the transition. Between March 1943, and March 1944, the Red Cross received 4,920 requests for personal counseling from the families on base.

In addition to the counseling service, the Red Cross was authorized to offer small personal loans to the service men or their families. During 1943, the Red Cross made loans totaling $33,215.00 to the service men alone, not counting loans made to families. The Red Cross staff also trained the First Aid Instructors on the base, so a four-hour course in First Aid could be offered year-around as part of the routine coursework for all base personnel.[32]

The Red Cross assigned a Recreation Director to the hospital, and the Red Cross Gray Ladies Corps assisted with the welfare, social services and recreation duties at the hospital. The "Gray Ladies" volunteers were so-called because of the gray color of their uniforms, not the color of their hair. They were usually wives or family members of the soldiers. The Red Cross established a Convalescent Training service, which encouraged the volunteers to help the patients with their convalescent care. The convalescent training expanded quickly with the help of the Gray Ladies.

In 1944, a separate Red Cross recreation building was opened and became the center for patient recreation. The new building housed an auditorium and stage, offices for the Red Cross Field Director and Assistant, a library, living quarters for the staff, and rooms for visiting relatives of seriously ill patients. Red Cross volunteers provided movies, quiz programs, music and parties for patients and their families. Many nationally famous musicians and other entertainment people gave programs at the Red Cross building, as did as local entertainers. At Christmas time, the Garden Clubs of Houston and the Gray Ladies decorated the entire hospital and helped with Christmas parties and festivities. Through the Red Cross, civilian families invited patients to have dinner with them, and local individuals donated tickets to concerts, wrestling matches, rodeos, and plays to the patients and staff.

Community Support

Many Houston families invited servicemen to their homes on the weekends during World War II. Humble Oil vice president Herman Pressler was the head of the Red Cross in Houston, and oversaw the branch at Ellington Field. He and his wife Elsie invited officers and enlisted men from Ellington to Sunday dinners on a regular basis.[33] One year, oilman Hugh Roy Cullen invited every serviceman who had no place to go for Christmas dinner to come to his house, and the response was overwhelming.

Bernardo "Barney" Weismantel was a tailor selling shirts at the Montgomery Ward store in Houston when World War II began. He had no commercial equipment and no employees, but he decided he wanted to bid on the tailoring concession at Ellington Field. The job was to dry clean and tailor all the men's uniforms- it was a big contract, and there were three of the big name cleaners in town bidding on it. Colonel Reid, the base commander, was impressed with Barney's tailoring and his willingness to put all he had into the job he helped Barney through the bidding procedures. Against considerable odds, Mr. Weismantel won the contract. Once the notice that "Barney the Tailor" had won the contract was posted on the base, men lined up all around the block and Mr. Weismantel suddenly had more work than he could do. There were thousands of men coming in, and every one needed his uniforms tailored to fit. Barney rented an office in downtown Houston, and hired some of his friends to help. Eventually he and his wife bought a house near River Oaks, where they entertained any and all soldiers who dropped by. They grilled steaks out in the yard and had coolers of cold beer. On any given weekend, the family might have ten visitors, or they might have sixty. Many slept over on the porch and patio outside when the weather was good, or inside all over the floors when the weather was cold or rainy. Barney and his wife hosted servicemen every weekend all four years of the war. His home was their second home. It became a tradition for the visiting soldiers to carve their initials in the Weismantel's dining room table, and by the end of the war when Ellington closed down, the entire table was covered with initials and notes. The table was kept by his son for a number of years, then donated to a museum in Ohio.[34]

Business owners in Houston supported the war effort by doing what they could for the servicemen. The Soldiers Service Bureau was established in office space donated by Houston business woman Mellie Esperson. The Service Bureau kept track of events being held in town for the servicemen, and Houston's hospitality was full of enticements for the soldiers and sailors on the weekends. Churches held special Sunday services for the servicemen and invited them to bingo games, church socials and picnics. Charitable organizations like the YMCA and the USO offered inexpensive places to stay, help with correspondence, family counseling, legal work, and other important services. Dances headed the list of the most popular things for the servicemen. Newspaper articles from the times suggest there were plenty of dances to attend. One article from *The Houston Post* for January, 1942, listed a tea dance for up one thousand soldiers at the Corps Club, another dance at the City Recreation Department, and still others at the YWCA, the Jewish Welfare Board, the USO, and the YMCA. Open houses in private homes where soldiers and sailors could drop by on a Saturday or Sunday afternoon for cookies and punch or doughnuts and coffee were also popular.[35]

The Corps Club was a canteen club run by Mrs. Elizabeth Harris and a group of "Gold Star Mothers." The designation of "Gold Star Mother" was begun in World War I. On May 28, 1918, President Wilson approved a suggestion made by the Women's Committee of the Council of National Defenses that, instead of wearing conventional mourning apparel for relatives who died in the service of their country, American women should wear a black band on the left arm with a gold star for each member of the family who had given his life for the nation. In the years following, service flags were displayed from homes, places of business, churches, schools, etc., to indicate the number of members of the family or organizations who were serving in the Armed Forces or who had died in the service. These service flags had a deep blue star for each living member in the service and a gold star for each member who had died. A mother displaying this flag has the highly respected designation of being a "Gold Star Mother."

The Ellington Field Post Band

Whether played by fife and drum, bagpipes, bugle, or full marching band, music has always been a part of military life. In hundreds of wars and conflicts, soldiers were taught to march to the cadence of a drum; armies were directed to charge into battle or retreat from it by a bugle playing. Fallen heroes were 'piped home" with bagpipes and buried to the mournful tune of "Taps". Even today, each branch of the service has a full military band which plays at important military affairs, recruitment drives, and public functions. The first Ellington Field Band was organized in 1918 by Captain William J. Dunn. Dunn arrived at Ellington Field in December of 1917, as the commander of the 120th Aero Squadron. Besides his military duties, he was in charge of the social functions as the field and the Liberty Bond drives. He enlisted the help of Sgt. R.L. Estabrook as Band Leader, and they assembled a 27 piece orchestra. The band played at all the dances on the post, and participated in military ceremonies and parades in downtown Houston.

On September 15, 1941, twenty-five enlisted men[36] stationed at Ellington Field organized a band under the baton of Staff Sgt. John Buchanan. Fifteen days later, the War Department authorized a post band for Ellington. Four experienced bandsmen were transferred in from Camp Hulen, Texas to help mold the fledgling organization into a first-class Military Band. On Armistice Day, November 11, 1941, the band made its first public appearance at the Armistice Day parade in Houston. It was accompanied by the Women's Army Corps Detachment from Ellington Field, which had been selected to carry the Post Colors as the Honor Unit in the Parade.

Because there were so many servicemen stationed in and around Houston, the USO, YMCA and YWCA collaborated to provide dances every Saturday night for the soldiers. The Ellington Air Force band's performances grew in number as they began to provide music for these dances. In August of 1942, the War Department re-designated the Air Force Band, under the command of Capt. Joe B. McDonald, as the 319th Air Forces Band, Ellington Field, Texas.

In September of 1942, the United States Government started a vast recruiting program for the Army Air Corps and sent the band on the road to generate patriotism and enthusiasm. Capt. Raymond Pearson was in charge of the first recruiting tour, and during the month of September, the Ellington Band played in 27 cities in East Texas. The first tour was so successful that the band was sent out again for the month of October to visit more towns in East Texas and Arkansas. The band set up headquarters in Little Rock, and played performances twice a day at a central location in the city. Radio Station KARK also broadcast their performances several times. The second trip was so successful that each member of the band received a commendation from Colonel Walter H. Reid, the Commanding Officer of Ellington Field, for his part in the recruiting drive.

By 1943, one twenty-eight piece band was no longer enough to provide the music for the many military occasions. The War Department activated the 411th Army Air Force Band into service at Ellington Field, combined the two bands and assigned Capt. Robert Soderberg as commanding officer of both bands. After much rearranging, Capt. Soderberg managed to acquire a barracks for the band members, and turned the old recreation hall into a rehearsal and administration building for the bands.

Capt. Soderberg had been the director of the AAF Band at Randolph Field, in San Antonio, Texas, and had worked with other Army bands for the past twenty-four years. Musicians in the Army considered him to be one of the best band leaders in his field. Many of the musicians had played with well-known dance bands and orchestras before their induction into the Army, so two more dance bands were organized. One played at the Officer's Club on base every Saturday night, and the other played for the Cadet Club at the Lamar Hotel in Houston.

In mid-summer, a recruitment campaign began for prospective soldiers among the 17-year-old young men in the area. To acquaint them with life in the Army, they were invited to an open house at Ellington Field on July 4, 1943. Mr. Ernst Hoffman of the Houston Symphony was the guest conductor of the day. The band continued assisting the 17-year-old recruiting program through the months of July and September by giving concerts in Houston.

In November, the band set off on a recruiting drive again, this time to enlist women for the Women's Army Corps. The military band made a tour of cities in southern and eastern Texas while the orchestra played three times a day at the WAC recruiting Post at the corner of Main and Rusk Streets in Houston. The WAC recruiting tour continued through December then came back to the base for the holidays. On Jan. 24, 1944, the Army re-designated the 319th Band as the 619th Army Band, and the 411th AAF Band as the 711th Army Band, then reassigned both bands to the Adjutant General Department.[37]

End Notes

[1] Col. Walter H. Reid, interview by Lt. T.R. Havins, in *The History of Ellington Field 1941-1944* (Maxwell AFB: AFHRA, 2002) Microfilm, roll B2175.

[2] "History of Ellington Field", article on Houston Airport System Website at www.ci.houston.tx.us/has/efd_history.html.

[3] "Matagorda Island State Park and Wildlife Management Area", *Handbook of Texas Online*, www.tsha.utexas.edu/handbook/online/articles/view.

[4] R.A. Laird, interview by Lt. T.R. Havins, in *The History of Ellington Field, 1941-1944* (Maxwell AFB: AFHRA, 2002). Microfilm, roll B2175.

[5] "New Ellington Rises on Site of Old Field", *The Houston Press*, May 23,1941, 26.

[6] "*Historical Background—Ellington Air Force Base, Houston, Texas,*" no author, paper supplied by the Houston Airport System Operations Office, Ellington Field, 3.

[7] Although Reid was stationed at Ellington, his name does not appear on the "Directory of Officers, Cadets and Nursed of Ellington Field on page 193 of the book, *Ellington 1918*, perhaps because the publication date preceded his assignment.

[8] Thomas E. Alexander, *The Wings of Change. The Army Air Force Experience in Texas During World War II* (McWhiney Foundation Press, Abilene, 2003), 64.

[9] Ibid.

[10] "Ellington Field Accessible by Railroad and Highway," *Houston Chronicle*, Jun 6,1940.

[11]"New Ellington Rises on Site of Old Field", *Houston Press*, May 23,1941, 26.

[12] "Last Big Push On to Complete Ellington Field, Air Academy Will Probably Open May 1," *Houston Post,* April 4, 1941, 1.

[13] *"History of the Pilot School, Ellington Field, Texas, 1940-1 March 1944*" (Maxwell AFB: AFHRA,2002) Microfilm, roll B2175,.6.

[14] Ibid., 8.

[15] "*History of the Pilot School, Ellington Field, Texas, 1940-1 March 1944.*" (Maxwell AFB: AFHRA, 2002) Microfilm, roll B2175, 12.

[16] Ibid., 11.

[17] *Charles E. Yeager Biography* (Edwards Air Force Base, Ca: Officce of Public Affairs, 1993), 1.

[18] *History of the Pilot School, Ellington Field, Texas, 1940-1 March 1944* (Maxwell AFB: AFHRA, 2002) Microfilm, roll B2175, 15.

[19] Ibid.,18.

[20] Lt. Joseph S. Fyfe, *History of the Station Hospital at Ellington Field, Texas, 21 May 1941-7 December 1941*(Maxwell AFB: AFHRA, 2002), Microfilm, roll B2175, 17.

[21] Robert G. Hahn, interview by Lt. T.R. Havins, in *The History of Ellington Field, April 1941-1 March 1944,* 2 vols. (Maxwell AFB: AFHRA, 2002), Microfilm, roll B2175.

[22] Fyfe, 2.

[23] Ibid., 6.

[24] Ibid., 5.

[25] Ibid., 6.

[26]Ibid., 17.

[27] Ibid.

[28] Ibid., 12.

[29] Interview, Vaughan J. Radcliffe by author, April 26, 200, at this home in Channelview, Texas.

[30] Ibid.,16.

[31] Camp Surgeon's Report, 1943, in *The History of Ellington Field, 1941-1944*. (Maxwell AFB: AFHRA, 2002). Microfilm roll B2175, 16,27, 29.

[32] Havins, 2, 226-228.

[33] *Houston Chronicle,* March 29, 2005.

[34] Mr.Guy Weismantel, interviewed by Kathryn Morrow, transcript of tape recording 20 May 2003, Houston , Texas.

[35] *The Houston Post,* January 8, 1942.

[36] For a list of the members of the band, see Appendix 3.

[37] *History of the 619th and 711th Army Bands* (Maxwell AFB: AFHRA, 2002) Microfilm, roll B2176.

CHAPTER III

Black Soldiers at Ellington Field: Desegregation in the Military

One of the major turning points within the civil rights movement in the United States was the increasing effort of the Federal Government to find ways to enforce a standard of integration across the country. This effort began during the Presidency of Franklin Delano Roosevelt and continued into the 1970's. One key piece of legislation was Executive order 9981, issued by President Harry S. Truman in 1948, which mandated desegregation in all of the branches of the military services. Black soldiers became a significant presence in the United States Army during the Civil War, and as the United States entered into World War I and II, the numbers of blacks in the military increased dramatically. It became increasingly unacceptable to offer men equal opportunities to die for their country, and then deny them equal opportunities to live in it.

All-black units were a unique part of military history in Texas, which was at the same time a southern state and a western frontier. After the Civil War, congress created the Ninth and Tenth Cavalry and Twenty Fourth and Twenty Fifth Infantry Regiments to recognize the contributions and valiant service of the black soldiers. These became known over time as the "Buffalo Soldiers". These regiments were the only units that allowed blacks to have a place in the Regular Army until 1944.[1] The Twenty Fourth Infantry Regiment was stationed at Fort McKavett, Texas, and helped garrison several posts in western Texas and along the Rio Grande until 1880. In the early 1900's, the all-black Twenty Fourth and Twenty Fifth Infantry Regiments of the United States Army were primarily stationed out on the frontier in western Texas, Indian Territory and Utah, where the vision of black men wearing uniforms, carrying guns, and earning respect could be kept far removed from the general population. The Twenty Fourth Regiment was also involved in military actions associated with American colonial enterprise in distant places like the Philippines and Cuba, which gave the black soldiers an opportunity to prove themselves in battle. After 1900, as the United States approached World War I, most of the white population of America still believed that blacks were biologically and mentally inferior. Two racial stereotypes were especially damaging: that blacks lacked the ability to absorb much knowledge, and that black soldiers performed well only under the supervision of white officers. This general attitude affected blacks in the military in several significant ways. Army officers generally accepted these presumed limitations and their decisions were shaped by them, which limited the types of jobs and promotions offered to black soldiers; and, since most of the Army's training bases were in the South, continual contact with civilians who held these attitudes reinforced the idea that these concepts were correct.[2]

The buildup of military bases near cities across the country during World War I brought black soldiers into closer proximity to white populations. The public could no longer ignore the existence of black soldiers because of their increasing presence in the communities. Their military status also made them an influence not controlled by the hierarchy of local law. They were moved around by order of the Federal Government, whether or not they were wanted by the local government. Racism increased, and the discrimination, segregation and antipathy experienced by black soldiers during and after World War I created a resentment that would fuel the beginnings of black activism for the next two decades. In Texas history, the Houston Riot of 1917 was one of the saddest results of pent-up resentment that led to conflict, resistance, and fatal gunfire.

In the late summer of 1917, the War Department ordered the Third Battalion of the Twenty Fourth Infantry to guard the construction site at Camp Logan, which was being built on the outskirts of Houston, Texas. From the time the black troops arrived, the white community of Houston made no effort to hide its resentment of their presence and the black soldiers of the unit faced racial discrimination when they received passes to go into the city. Racial insults and abusive epithets were repeatedly hurled at them, and they were denied access to recreational facilities that were open to white soldiers. A majority of the men had been raised in the South and were familiar with segregation, but as army servicemen they expected equal treatment.[3]

Those individuals responsible for keeping order, especially the police, streetcar conductors, and public officials, viewed the presence of black soldiers as a threat to racial harmony. Black soldiers were willing to abide by the legal restrictions imposed by segregated practices, but they resented the manner in which the laws were enforced. They disliked the Jim Crow restrictions that required them to stand in the rear of streetcars when vacant seats were available in the "white" section and closed restaurants, public toilets, and other city facilities to them. The military officers recognized the plight of the enlisted men, but did little to alert civil authorities to the growing tensions.[4]

On August 24, 1917, an armed conflict arose between men from Camp Logan and Houston policemen in which twelve white civilians, four white policemen, and four black soldiers were killed. On August 25th, the army put the entire Third Battalion aboard a train back to New Mexico, and within three days, the Texas legislature passed a law forbidding the military to bring any more black soldiers into the state. The War Department subsequently indicted 118 black soldiers. Nineteen of the black soldiers were summarily hanged before a judicial review could take place, and sixty-three received life sentences. Two white policemen were charged but released, and no civilians were ever charged.[5]

Treatment of Black Soldiers Between World War I and World War II

In the years between World War I and World War II, there was much discussion in black political circles about the rampant racial prejudice faced by black soldiers on and off military bases. President Franklin Delano Roosevelt's[6] administration (1932-1945) was pressured by black leaders to end the flagrant discrimination and segregation faced by black inductees into the military. In 1938, the Army adopted a policy that required the proportion of blacks in the military to be equal to the proportionate number of blacks in the national population, i.e., nine to ten percent, but the number of blacks who remained in the military continued to drop. By 1939, the number of blacks in uniform declined to fewer than 4,000.[7] The need for manpower in the face of World War II compelled the armed services and the Roosevelt administration to confront the unfairness of subjecting men to wartime service, then denying them equal workplace privileges and progression in rank. On September 14, 1940, congress passed the Burke-Wadsworth bill providing for the military draft, which was signed into law as the Selective Service Act. This act called for the registration of all men between the ages of twenty-one and thirty-five and the induction of 800,000 draftees into the armed forces. Section 304(a) stated "there shall be no discrimination against any person on account of race or color". Blacks could now serve in all the branches of the armed services. How they would be allowed to serve was still an open question.

Segregation was a firmly established American law, and the Selective Service Act did not broach the subject of segregation directly. Consequently, as the armed forces complied with the requirements of the Act, all-black units were formed, and black soldiers were frequently assigned to service units.[8] Since black soldiers were assigned to black training units, these units first had to be formed and staffed, which stalled progress of drafting blacks into the armed forces. Furthermore, although all branches of the armed forces were now open to blacks, the Army was the only branch that utilized the Selective Service draft. The Navy relied on volunteers and allowed blacks to serve only as messmen, and the Marine Corps did not take blacks at all. At this point, of course, the Air Force had not been established as a separate military force. This left only the Army to fulfill the population percentage (10.6%) of blacks in the armed forces until 1943.[9]

In 1942, the War Department decided to activate four black infantry divisions and supporting units in an attempt to solve the problems of absorbing a high enough number of blacks into the service to allow them to be placed in combat units. Separate but equal was not achieved in the armed forces during the first years of the war. There is some doubt that it could ever have been achieved, because the thinking behind military policy was focused on the *separate* to such an extent that efficiency, supposedly the major goal of the military, always subordinated to the goal of segregation. The effect of racial assumptions upon the utilization of Negro manpower seems obvious today. But those who made policy in the early 1940's identified their thinking with that of American society—white American society, to be sure, but what American Negroes thought did not seem so important at the time.[10]

The paradox of building a segregated military force to fight the racist ideology of Hitler was not lost on black soldiers, or eventually, even the War Department. Black soldiers like Amzie Moore (1912-) endured racism on a daily basis. Amzie Moore was born and raised in rural Mississippi. He grew up largely insulated within totally black communities and did not experience the full weight of segregation until he was drafted into the Army in 1942. After being shipped from one racist, segregated post to another in the United Sates, he was shipped overseas to Calcutta, India, only to find the military enlisted men's clubs were segregated even there. The Japanese saw the contradiction black American soldiers faced, and did not fail to use it as propaganda. The Japanese radio broadcasts reminded Black soldiers " that there was going to be no freedom for them, even after the war was over."[11]

It became Corporal Moore's job to counter this propaganda by giving lectures to Negro troops on their stake in the war. It was not surprising that he returned home a little angry. "Here I am being shipped overseas and I been segregated from this man whom I might have to save or he save my life. I didn't fail to tell it."… He returned home to Cleveland, Mississippi, in 1946 to find that local whites had organized a home guard to protect themselves against returning Negro veterans who were presumed to have acquired a taste for white women. A number of Blacks were killed, murders that Moore believed were intended to intimidate returning servicemen. After an FBI investigation, the murders stopped.[12]

As a result of such violent reactions at home, in August of 1942, the War Department established the Advisory Committee on Negro Troop Policies.[13] William Hastie, the civilian Aide to the Secretary of War, was so frustrated by the lack of progress made in easing the racial problems faced by black soldiers that he resigned in 1943. His resignation had some impact on the policies of the Advisory Committee: the plan for a separate black Army Air Force officers school was dropped; black doctors were given training in aviation medicine; technical training for black troops was expanded; and the barriers to the promotion of black officers were removed. The Committee also succeeded in informing the Army General Staff and the War Department of the extent of the racial problems within the military. In 1943 and 1944, the Committee established good relations between the black press and the War Department, encouraged the arrangement of equal transportation for black soldiers to and from the bases where they were stationed, and began to publicize the contributions of the black soldiers in the war effort, most notably in the film, *The Negro Soldier*. In 1946, the Committee also cooperated in producing pamphlets designed to inform officers of the War Department's official policy regarding the treatment of black soldiers; that black soldiers should be judged as individuals and used according to their abilities. [14] The most important action the Advisory Committee took, and the one with the most potential for directly affecting segregation on military bases, came in July, 1944. The Committee issued a directive that all facilities on military posts would be used without restriction due to race. This meant post exchanges, recreation halls, hospitals and officer's and enlisted clubs and movie theaters on bases would be integrated. This directive had little effect on bases that already had separate buildings in place for these facilities, and in such cases, segregation continued on as before.

Military bases often tended to be only as informed and enthusiastic about integration as their commanding officers were. Since most of the training bases had been built in the South, and the prevailing attitude was to place white officers with "experience with blacks", i.e., southerners, in command of black units, black inductees were often placed in an intolerable situation. Even when the commanding officer insisted on equal treatment and respect for all the soldiers under his command, there were no such guarantees off base. Only the urgent need for manpower towards the end of the war and an impending presidential election secured real changes in the status of blacks in the military. [15]

> The urgent need for soldiers to fight abroad and for wage-earners to forge an 'arsenal of democracy' at home convinced a flood of African-Americans to leave the South. Mechanized cotton pickers shrunk the need for agrarian labor just as the lure of good jobs in war industries sapped the will to stay in the fields. Metropolises from Los Angeles to New York filled up with dark-skinned residents-and , after the war, the flow persisted. Between 1940 and 1960, 4.5 million black men and women migrated out of Dixie...."[16]

Ironically, many of the blacks who moved north and enlisted in the military were then stationed back on bases in the South.

At the end of World War II, the United States was now a leading force for democracy, but its own backward racial policies hampered its influence with emerging countries.[17] The number and increasing militancy of black voters was a significant political consideration. New tensions fueled by the return of black veterans who were no longer satisfied with the racial status quo and the resurgence of the Ku Klux Klan set the stage for a major change of direction. President Harry S. Truman[18] had a long history of supporting equal rights for all citizens, and was well familiar with the wartime grievances of black soldiers. As a Senator, Truman supported legislation to include blacks in the Civilian Pilot Training program, [19] organized a committee to investigate the extent of discrimination against minorities in defense contracts,[20] and supported the investigation of how segregation affected the opportunities of blacks in military service in a bill put forth by the *Pittsburgh Courier*.[21] In December of 1946, President Truman (1945-1952) appointed an Advisory Committee on Civil Rights to survey the status, difficulties, and needs of minority citizens. In January 1947, President Harry S. Truman called for a report from each branch of the military on their use and treatment of minorities in the service.[22] In an address to the Annual Conference of the National Association for the advancement of Colored People (NAACP) given on June 28, 1947, the President said:

> ...I should like to talk to you briefly about civil rights and human freedom. It is my deep conviction that we have reached a turning point in the long history of our country's efforts to guarantee freedom and equality to all our citizens.... And when I say all Americans—I mean all Americans.... The extension of civil rights today means, not protection of the people against the Government, but protection of the people by the Government.... There is no justifiable reason for discrimination because of ancestry, or religion, or race, or color.... Many of our people still suffer the indignity of the insult, the harrowing fear of intimidation, and, I regret to say, the threat of physical injury and mob violence.... We cannot wait another decade or another generation to remedy those evils...we can no longer afford the luxury of a leisurely attack upon prejudice and discrimination...we cannot...await the growth of a will to action in the slowest state of the most backward community....[23]

Truman's Committee investigated the treatment and policies of all branches of the armed forces, then reported back. On July 26, 1948, Truman issued Executive Order 9981[24] that eliminated, at least on paper, the concept of segregation on US military bases and posts.

Mandating desegregation on military bases allowed the Federal Government to set an example of fostering civil rights in a controlled environment. The dynamics of race relations on a military base were different from other populations for at least four reasons: 1.) There was top-down pressure from the government to give equal pay, status and promotion to all male soldiers, regardless of race. 2.) Military rank hierarchy forced respect for officers and non-commissioned officers, regardless of color, especially for those with combat experience. 3.) The population of a base had little to do with where the base was located. Thus, a base located in the South might be largely populated by soldiers and officers from northern or eastern cities, or vice versa. There was an inevitable exposure to wider racial attitudes and views on civil rights than experienced in more monolithic local populations. 4.) The population on military bases, especially during wartime, was in a constant state of flux, so the mixture of people, attitudes, and problems was constantly being changed.

Encouraging desegregation in the communities around military bases was another battle, but it was a controllable battle. The Federal Government eventually used the "big stick" of economic prosperity to enforce desegregation and fair treatment. Communities impacted by the presence of a large military base became dependent on the revenue generated by that base. It was not uncommon for hundreds of new businesses to spring up around a new base. Those businesses necessarily complied with military regulations and standards or suffered being declared "off limits" to military personnel and their paychecks. One example of the federal government's no-tolerance attitude towards segregation that was specific to the economy of Houston involved the Space program. In 1964, NASA was receiving approximately 8,000 requests a year for tours of the Manned Spacecraft Center near Ellington, as well as speaking programs, exhibits, and films from the MSC. Paul Haney, then public affairs official for the MSC said that all requests would be screened to make sure the programs would be available to all, regardless of race. Schools and other organizations wanting educational programs from the MSC had to assure them that Negro students would not be barred from attending the programs or black schools from requesting programs.[25] To put this into clearer historical perspective, it was not until 1963 that "Negroes" were allowed to enroll at Texas A& M University, [26] and not until 1964 that the City of Houston dropped the "race" question from its employee application.[27]

Blacks in the Military in Texas

One black officer's experience with the discrepancies between military and local civil rights is not as familiar to students of black history as his later experience with racial discrimination in athletics, but deserves mention in this book:

> One morning in July of 1944, a civilian bus driver at Fort Hood, Texas, ordered a black army lieutenant to 'get to the back of the bus where the colored people belong.' The lieutenant refused, arguing that the military had recently ordered its buses desegregated. MPs came and took him into custody. Four weeks later, the black officer went on trial for insubordination. If convicted by the court martial, he faced a dishonorable discharge- which would have crippled his job opportunities for the rest of his life. The lieutenant's name was Jackie Robinson. Three years later, Robinson would don the uniform of the Brooklyn Dodgers to become the first African-American man in the twentieth century to play major league baseball. Robinson's bold defiance of racial custom, his appeal to Federal authority, and his acquittal by that military court in 1944 all indicated that significant changes were in spin. World War II was a watershed in African-American history, raising the hopes of people who, with their children, would build the massive black freedom movement of the 1960's.[28]

During World War II, the majority of the 80,000 black Texans who saw military service in World War II were assigned to segregated units that were still commanded by white officers. Most of them received basic military training in camps located in Texas and other Southern states with entrenched segregation. Separate and inferior facilities for African-American soldiers existed at many military installations.[29] Understanding the complex forces behind the effort to desegregate the military is easier if viewed through a representative example, such as Ellington Air Force Base near Houston, Texas.

Black Experiences at Ellington Field

There were no black soldiers stationed at Ellington Field during World War I, because Ellington Field was an aviation training base, and there were no black soldiers in the Air Service. One black soldier who fought his way through several wars and came to Ellington Field after his discharge from the military was Sgt. Hugh McElroy (1884-1971). Sgt. McElroy, in his own words was "always crazy about soldiering." He served with Teddy Roosevelt in Cuba during the Spanish-American War (1899-1902), fought in the Philippine Insurrection (1898-1899), was a soldier in the punitive expedition against Pancho Villa in Mexico under Gen. Pershing (1916), and he served again in World War I (1914-1918). After his valiant service in World War I, Pres. George Clemenceau of France awarded him the Croix de Guerre for his heroic action on the front lines in France while attached to the Seventh French Army. However, the United States, his own country, refused to recognize Sgt. McElroy's wartime contribution. Despite a letter from his commanding officer that outlined Sgt. McElroy's repeated bravery while his unit was under fire, all the War Department would accord Sgt. McElroy was a letter to accompany his General Orders out of the service.[30]

79th Aviation Squadron at Ellington Field, from Army Air Forces Training Command Yearbook

After his military service ended in 1927, McElroy came to Houston. During World War II, he was the head janitor at Ellington Field. During this period, Sgt. McElroy said he talked to every "colored" soldier that was stationed at Ellington about the benefits of military service: "I told them the colored people would get just as much benefit from winning the war as the white people would." [31] He also worked at recruiting stations until retiring permanently. He participated in World War II war bond drives as both a speaker and poster model. He was the first African-American whose picture appeared as an advertisement for United States War Bonds. He was honored at the 1968 HemisFair in San Antonio with a life-size portrait in the Texas pavilion, underneath which was a recounting of his military record. Sgt. McElroy died December 29, 1971, and a detachment from Fort Sam Houston was sent to bury him with full military honors.[32]

Information on the conditions for black soldiers at Ellington in the decade prior to the Executive Order of 1948 was very limited, but the few notes that existed were intriguing. It is almost certain, however, that adding more than 1,400 black men and their families to the local population could have been a key ingredient in a recipe for conflict. The previously referenced Houston Riot of 1917, which involved black military soldiers from Camp Logan and white police officers, was an example of the type of rapidly escalating racial situation that could occur.[33] However, interviews with white and black soldiers and other research indicated that racial conflict on the base at Ellington during World War II was minimal.

It is possible that the reason for this reported lack of conflict was that many of the typical ingredients for racial conflict were absent from Ellington Field. For instance, whereas white men enlisted for aviation training and were shipped to Ellington from all over the country, most of the black soldiers came to Ellington from local recruitment. Almost all of the men in the 79th Aviation squadron were from Texas or Louisiana. These men would have been very familiar with the racial protocols in Texas, and adept at living within the system. Additionally, the living conditions for black soldiers at Ellington were not inferior to that of white soldiers because all the buildings were newly built, and identical. Recreation halls, mess halls, hospital wards and other facilities were new as well, and there were separate facilities for the black soldiers. In addition to new barracks, one base report listed a "colored" NCO club, another referred to Post Exchange Branch #3 as the "Negro Exchange".[34] The main theater was in the recreation hall and there were two other areas for showing training films. One was in Section F of the 2517th Base unit (colored). There was no listing to indicate whether the athletic leagues, bowling alley, bands, glee club, chapels or guest houses were available to the black soldiers at special times, or were completely off-limits.[35]

Racial segregation was an accepted social norm for the times, and having the black soldiers segregated probably eliminated most opportunities for face to face confrontation. Indications of segregated units and facilities are found in a chart[36] showing the square footage, housing, seating, and cooking capacity for the buildings on the base in 1944. It may be helpful to realize that in a military society, officers and enlisted men have always had separate facilities. Even modern military bases have Officer's Housing and an Officer's Club, usually on a different part of the base than the Enlisted Housing and Enlisted Men's Club. In this sense, there has always been, and continues to be, a form of social segregation among all military personnel, even on modern bases.

The records from Ellington Field show housing for 349 white officers and warrant officers, and for 20 "colored" officers and warrant officers: 5,777 white enlisted men and 1,352 "colored" enlisted men. It also indicated mess hall seating capacity for 500 white officers and warrant officers, but none for "colored" officers, probably because the highest-ranking black soldier was Tsgt. Snowden McKinnon[37]. The white enlisted men and the "colored" enlisted men ate in separate mess halls, each in their own area of the base.

In the 1943 *Army Air Force Training Command Yearbook* for Ellington Field, there were photos of a Medical Detachment, "Colored" with fifteen men, as well as photos of the 79th Aviation Squadron with three white officers and 194 enlisted men, and one page of casual photos of these men in various activities.[38] The Camp Surgeon's notes for 1943 previously referenced in this paper also had several notes on "colored" enlisted men at Ellington. Among the notes on communicable disease prevention and control was the statement: "The colored organization on this field now has two men who have attended…school at Tuskegee Institute. They are materially aiding us in their organization."[39] The use of the words "their organization" indicated that the "colored enlisted men" were in a segregated unit.

The 1945 history of the 2517th Base Unit noted that Squadron F, made up of white officers and "Negro" enlisted men, was the general service unit, and that housing was provided for 2,721 white enlisted men, and 464 "Negro" enlisted men.[40] The most intriguing note in the historical files came during the period when the base was used as a "separation base" during 1945, at the end of World War II. Military personnel were shipped to Ellington from other bases to be transitioned out of the service. The number of personnel at the base varied widely during 1945 as units came and left. Facilities were consolidated and buildings closed. During November and December, 1945, the Consolidated (negro) Mess was closed for fumigation and inspection by the Post Sanitary Engineer, and the Station Food Service Supervisor decided to keep the building closed, "in view of its impending consolidation with the white mess."[41] This period also saw the WAC Mess consolidated into the Hospital Mess, so by the end of December, 1945, there were two Officers Messes, a Hospital Mess seating officers, enlisted men and WACS, and a consolidated enlisted Mess, seating both black and white enlisted men.[42] This historic merging took place a full three years before the President of the United States mandated desegregation in the military.

As mentioned, recruiters at Ellington Field placed advertisements seeking black enlistees for the 79th Aviation Squadron. The aforementioned Tech Sgt. Snowden McKinnon was working as a detective for the Pinkerton Detective Agency in Houston when he saw a newspaper recruitment ad that advertised for blacks with clerical or typing experience to join an aviation squadron at Ellington Field. He had attended Hughes Business School in Houston and had the required skills. In his own words, "I had an assignment in Galveston, with Pinkerton...and I told my boss I think I'll answer this ad in the paper and go into Ellington Field, and be a G.I." His boss at Pinkerton gave him a letter of recommendation to take to Headquarters. "So I took it to the base, and they gave me 18197021, my serial number." Snowden McKinnon was now Sgt. Snowden McKinnon, soldier. He enlisted at Ellington and served in the 79th Aviation Squadron from 1940 to 1944.[43]

Mr. McKinnon recounted his memories of life as a black soldier at Ellington Field in interviews during 2003. He was by then 92 years old, and a retired Minister for the First Presbyterian Church in Dallas, Texas. According to him, most of the black enlisted men were from Texas and Louisiana.[44] Like Mr. McKinnon, many answered the ad not just for a chance to contribute to the war effort, but also for the practical considerations of a decent, long-term job, steady paycheck and the G.I. benefits that would later pay their way through college. They knew they would face segregation and would be barred from becoming officers, but most of the men who came to Ellington were from Texas and Louisiana, and had lived with segregation all their lives.

The men's experiences on base were very similar to all enlisted men. They were issued uniforms, trained for their various duties, drilled in formation, worked wherever they were needed on base, and lived in barracks.

When asked about their treatment by the white enlisted men and officers on base, Mr. McKinnon replied that Col. Reid was a good base commander and a fair man who ran a tight base, and that there were seldom any acts of outright aggression or prejudice shown to them. When there were, he said, "We just let it go. We were proud to be able to serve, and to do anything we could to keep those pilots flying."

Men from the 79th Aviation Squadron from Army Air Force Training Command Yearbook

The fact that their barracks and other facilities were apart at one end of the base was a normal aspect of life at that time. Like all soldiers, when the work day was over, the men gathered at the exchange to chat, at the recreation hall to play ping pong, or at the library. At the end of the week, the black enlisted men went into Houston, but instead of going to the Rice Hotel like the aviation cadets, they went to the homes of members of black churches where they would be housed and fed, and where they could relax. The squadron also developed a very good men's chorus that sang in churches all over Houston. Eventually, the group was put on recruitment tours in Texas and Louisiana as the Ellington Field Negro Men's Chorus. Under such circumstances, the men formed long-lasting friendships and bonds of trust. Many of the men remained in touch through the years after the war. As Mr. McKinnon reviewed the pictures of the men in the 79th Aviation Squadron, he remembered something about each one of them: "This one had a beautiful tenor voice, this one was a great pitcher, this one used to tell me jokes that made me laugh! Oh, we were proud to serve!"

Tsgt. Snowden McKinnon seated at desk surrounded by men of the 79TH Aviation Squadron. Courtesy of Snowden F. McKinnon. White officer is 1ST Lt. Adrian Schroeder Army Air Force Training Command Yearbook

Men from the 79th Aviation Squadron Enjoying Recreation from Army Air Force Training Command Yearbook

Michael S. Sherry, in his book, *In the Shadow of War*, referred to the racial composition of the American Armed Forces in the late 1960's and 1970's:

> ...moreover, at a time of shrinking federal efforts to foster racial equality, the military loomed as a lonely bastion of progress, even though the inequalities persisted...Many male and female African-Americans continued to look to military service for education, heightened status, and upward job mobility.... Black's share of the military's enlisted ranks rose to 18.4 percent by 1978...[45]

The progress of integration in the Air Force was apparent from the photographs in the various squadron histories from Ellington Air Force Base. In the 1943 Air Training Command book, the photo pages of the individual black soldiers in their segregated squadrons were towards the back of the book, and their recreational activity photos were grouped together on a separate single page. By 1950, there appear to be black soldiers included in almost all the squadrons of the 3605th Navigation Training Wing—the Air Police, Installation, Food Service, Air Base Group, and the 722 Air Force Band. The men ranked from Private First Class to Master Sergeant. There did not appear to be any black officers or instructors, but there were black air cadets, and one black pilot, Captain Richard G. Stiverson, in the 3607th Training Squadron.[46]

By the end of World War II, the Federal Government had achieved only a minimal impact on how individual cities or states handled their racial issues, but they had begun to recognize the economic pressures that could be applied on and around the military bases that were scattered all over the country. Military bases were separate, self- contained cities with their own grocery stores, central shopping, gasoline stations and schools. Military personnel were governed by an additional layer of rules, and subject to military discipline. The presence of a large military base was often the key economic factor in the growth and stability of surrounding communities, which gave the Federal Government a powerful economic stick to wield in enforcing compliance with civil rights issues and equal treatment for black military personnel and their families off base as well as on base.

The National Security Act of 1947 created the United States Air Force as a separate service. On September 26, 1947, the Secretary of Defense ordered the personnel of the Army Air Forces (AAF) transferred from the Department of the Army to the Department of the Air Force and established as the United States Air Force (USAF). [47] Ellington Field became Ellington Air Force Base. In 1948, Ellington Air Force Base operated on a limited basis as an Air Force Reserve and Texas National Guard base, and in August of 1949, it experienced a rebirth as the only post-war United States Air Force navigation training school. The rebirth of Ellington Field caused much excitement in the surrounding communities, because the new program brought 2,000 to 3,000 permanent military and civilian personnel to the area, with a payroll of $1 million dollars.[48]

By the end of 1952, the Air Force had become the first branch of the armed services with no all-black components. "...Armed Forces integration provided the Negro with his first opportunity in 335 years to live in an integrated society."[49] This meant that not only were black soldiers working and eating alongside their white counterparts, but those families who lived on base were living in interracial neighborhoods, and their children were attending integrated schools on base, regardless of where that base was located. Many civilian neighborhoods and schools took much longer to integrate.[50] By the middle of the 1950's, the segregation on Ellington Air Force Base had ended. Lt. Robert Clark, who was a pilot trainee in the 3605th Navigator Training Wing at Ellington in 1956-1957, remembered that there were black students and enlisted men at the base then, and that there was no question of segregation. All the facilities- barracks, mess halls, movie theaters, etc. were integrated. Lt. Clark worked closely with the Base Commander, Col. Norman Callish, and did not remember any racial incidents at the base while he was there.[51]

Weldon Foster was a black enlisted man who served with the U.S. Army 82nd Airborne Division from 1968-1972. He enlisted in Louisiana, was subsequently stationed at military bases in North Carolina and Georgia, and served a 16-month tour of duty in Vietnam. Sgt. Foster's experiences were probably typical of other black soldiers of the time. Since he was stationed at bases in the South, where racist attitudes had historically been the most extreme and longest enduring, his military experiences should be a reasonable indicator of any lingering racism in the military. Sgt. Foster encountered no incidences of segregation on any of the bases. He reported that there was no difference in the training he received as compared to that received by white soldiers and that all of the facilities on base were completely integrated. Sgt. Foster trained alongside white enlisted men, lived among white soldiers, and had full and equal access to recreational facilities, restaurants, theaters, and stores. Sgt. Foster did encounter racist remarks from a few individuals, but his overall military experience was positive enough to lead him to consider a career in the military. When asked by the interviewer if he would have recommended a military career to his sons now, he responded with a definite "Yes."[52] Family circumstances forced Sgt. Foster to leave the military after four years, but he enlisted in the Air Force Reserves and was stationed at Ellington Field.

In 1968, Columbia University undertook a study of the educational and career aspirations of black youth who had grown up in a military environment. One goal was to appraise the gains made from the military desegregation that had taken place two decades before, another was to determine what impact the gains had on these young people who had grown up in active military families. The respondents were black and white noncommissioned officers (NCOs) in the Air Force, who had dependent children aged fourteen years or older. A two part questionnaire was used; one part for the father to answer, one part for the child. According to the Air Force Military Personnel Center, in 1969 there were 7,000 black and 64,000 white NCOs who had children of the right age for the study stationed on bases in the continental United States. Although the response to the survey was lower than the study wished, the Air Force Sample Survey Officer concluded from the responses that they represented an appropriate cross section, evidencing "no bias by grade, time in service, or any other objective measure."[53] Men who enlisted in the Air Force prior to 1960 responded that they had experienced significant changes for the better in the racial atmosphere and opportunities for black men and women in the Air Force. Younger men who had enlisted after 1960, and who had come of age during the civil rights movement, were more negative in their responses and tended to focus on the areas that still needed improvement.

End Notes

[1] Marvin Fletcher, *The Black Soldier and Officer in the United States Army, 1891-1917* (Columbia, University of Missouri Press, 1974), 21.

[2] Ibid., 154, 155.

[3] Jack D. Foner, *Blacks and the Military in American History* (New York: Praeger Publishers, 1974), 115; Robert V. Haynes, *A Night of Violence: The Houston Riot of 1917* (Baton Rouge: Louisiana State University Press, 1976), 64-113.

[4] Haynes, *A Night of Violence: The Houston Riot of 1917.*

[5] Haynes, 322, 323.

[6] Roosevelt (1882-1945)

[7] Foner, 131.

[8] Richard M. Dalfiume, *Desegregation of the U.S. Armed Forces: Fighting on Two Fronts 1939-1953* (Columbia: University of Missouri Press, 1969), 44-61.

[9] Ibid., 53.

[10] Dalfiume, 63.

[11] Charles M. Payne, as quoted in *I've Got The Light of Freedom*, (Berkeley: University of California Press, 1995), 33.

[12] Ibid., 30, 31.

[13] Dalfiume, 83.

[14] Dalfiume, 88; War Department Circular Number 124, titled "Utilization of Negro Manpower in the Postwar Army Policy", dated April 27, 1946, included these objectives: "...the development of leaders and specialists based on individual merit and ability.... Groupings of Negro units with white units in composite organizations will be accepted policy.... The Ultimate Objective: the effective use of all manpower...without regard to antecedents of race." Also called the Gillem Report. Because the report mentioned separate black units, it was the source of some confusion.

[15] Dalfiume, 89, 90.

[16] Maurice Isserman and Michael Kazin, *America Divided: The Civil War of the 1960's* (New York: Oxford University Press, 2000), 23.

[17] William A. Rutherford, "Jim Crow: A Problem in Diplomacy," *The Nation*, 175 (November 8, 1952), 428-429.

[18] Truman (1884-1972).

[19] Lee Nichols, *Breakthrough On the Color Front* (New York: Random House Publishers, 1954), 83.

[20] Harry S. Truman, M*emoirs, Vol. II.* 9 (Garden City: Doubleday & Company, Inc. 1955-1956), 182.

[21] Pittsburgh *Courier,* June 28,1941.

[22] Robert K. Carr, The President's Committee on Civil Rights, *Memorandum For the War Department*, April 14, 1947. www.trumanlibrary.org/whistlestop/study collections/desegregation/large/1947/.

[23] President Harry S. Truman, NAACP Address, June 28, 1947, 1-3.

[24] President Harry S. Truman, Executive Order No. 9981. "Establishing the President's Committee

On Equality of Treatment and Opportunity in the Armed Forces," July 26, 1948.

[25] *Houston Chronicle*, September 4, 1964.

[26] *The Houston Post,* July 16, 1963.

[27] *Houston Press*, January 27, 1964.

[28] Maurice Isserman and Michael Kazin, *America Divided, the Civil War of the 1960s* (New York: Oxford University Press, 2002), 23.

[29] "Texans in World War II." *The Handbook of Texas Online.* www.tsha.utexas.edu/handbook/online/articles/view/WW.

[30] "Hugh McElroy," in *The Handbook of Texas Online,* www.tsha.utexas.edu/handbook/online.

[31] *Houston Chronicle,* Oct. 6,1968, Sec. 3, 1.

[32] McElroy." *The Handbook of Texas Online.*

[33] "Houston Riot of 1917." *The Handbook of Texas Online.* www.tsha.utexas.edu/handbook/online/articles/view/WW.

[34] Exchange Council letter dated 12 February 1945, p. 17A. Copy courtesy of Ellington Field Base Historians' office.

[35] Ibid.

[36] *Album of Station Information, Ellington Field, Texas* (Maxwell AFB: AFHRA, 2002). Microfilm, roll B2175.

[37] For more information on Tsgt. McKinnon, see page 35.

[38] *Army Air Forces Training Command, Ellington Field, Texas* (Baton Rouge: Army and Navy Publishing Company of Louisiana, c. 1942). See Appendix Four for a list of the men in these two units.

[39] Camp Surgeon's Report, 1943, in *The History of Ellington Field, 1941-1944* (Maxwell AFB: AFHRA, 2002). Microfilm roll B2175, 7.

[40] *History of the 2517th Base Unit, 1 September-31 October 1945* (Maxwell AFB: AFHRA, 2002). Microfilm roll B2175, 7.

[41] Ibid., 8.

[42] Ibid., 9.

[43] Interview, Snowden McKinnon by author, August 30, 2003 at his home in Dallas, TX.

[44] *Army Air Forces Training Command, Ellington Field, Texas* (Baton Rouge: Army and Navy Publishing Company of Louisiana, c. 1942, pp. 74, 190-194).

[45] Michael S. Sherry, *In the Shadow of War: The United States Since the 1930s.* (New Haven: Yale University Press, 1995), 366.

[46] *Navigation School, Ellington Air Force Base 1950.* (Baton Rouge: A&N Pictorial Publishers, 1950).

[47] "Evolution of the Department of the Air force", Air Force History site at www.airforcehsitory.hq.af.mil/soi/evolution_of_the_departmen.htm.

[48] *Houston Chronicle*. August 8, 1949.

[49] Alice Yohalem and Quentin B. Ridgely, *Desegregation and Career Goals; Children of Air Force Families.* Praeger Studies in U.S. Economic, Social, and Political Issues, (New York: Praeger Publishers, 1974), 2.

[50] Ibid., 38.

[51] Lt. Robert Clark, telephone interview by author, April 24, 2003.

[52] Weldon Foster, interview by author, April 20, 2003, in home of author, Houston, TX.

[53] Yohalem and Ridgely, 4.

CHAPTER IV

Women at Ellington Field

Men were not the only ones who served their country during times of war. As early as 1918, women performed significant service to the men stationed at Ellington Field. Nurses were part of the original hospital staff, and nursed the servicemen tirelessly during the Spanish influenza epidemic when a separate infirmary was set up. After the beginning of World War I, The Young Women's Christian Association (YWCA) built almost one hundred "Hostess Houses" on or near military bases all across the country. These Houses provided a much-needed respite from the rigors of military training, and most importantly, gave the men a home away from home. It was a hospitable inn for the weary soldier. It was a place of relaxation, attention and hospitality, where rank meant nothing. A staff of women[1] lived in each house and put in long hours every day providing comfort, rest and a quiet environment for the men on base. Pictures of the Hostess House at Ellington Field in 1918 show a large Craftsman-style bungalow with a screened-in porch furnished with rocking chairs and a large front yard. Interior pictures show a large living room[2] with a fireplace, ceiling fans, comfortable chairs, musical instruments, books, magazines, and writing paper. The cafeteria provided simple, home-cooked meals complete with the salads and desserts rarely offered in military mess halls. The Hostess House included a quiet room for visits between family members and their sons, husbands, or fathers. An information desk kept an up-to-date file with the unit location of every soldier on base. In the first six months, the Ellington Field Hostess House entertained more than 55,000 guests and served more than 30,000 meals.[3] The only time the Hostess House closed was during the global Spanish influenza epidemic in 1918. During the time the Hostess House was closed, the staff worked alongside the Post hospital nurses[4] to care for the influenza victims in a special isolation unit built on base.

Hostess House of Ellington Field taken from Ellington 1918.

Military Wives

Military wives have a long tradition of service as well. They have donated thousands of hours of volunteer service in relief projects over the years. One of the longest-serving volunteer groups found on military bases everywhere was the Gray Ladies Corps mentioned previously. In February of 1943, thirty-six ladies began their volunteer training with the Red Cross on Ellington Field. At the Base Hospital, the Gray Ladies assembled a library of 1,600 volumes and maintained subscriptions to 54 magazines for use by the patients. They arranged for three entertainment programs a week during which entertainers like magicians, musicians and comedians went from ward to ward to perform. Once a week they prepared a birthday party complete with a cake and all the trimmings for the patients who had birthdays during the week. This was quite a treat during the wartime rationing of sugar, oils and fats. The Gray Ladies Corps offered handicraft classes like leather craft and weaving that were very popular with the men. They also presented each patient with a weekly bedside bouquet of flowers to brighten their rooms. Robert Wilkins, Red Cross Director, said of their service: "The Gray Ladies Corps at Ellington Field is one of the largest and best units in this section."[5]

Another volunteer group made up of the wives of officers and enlisted men was the Ellington Field Red Cross Surgical Dressing Branch. The women came in at varying times once or twice a week to make surgical dressings, and when the need for dressings increased, so did the assigned quotas for the volunteers. It was serious work. The quota for dressings for the Red Cross Unit of Ellington for the month of May, 1943, was 32,500.[6] According to an interview with Mrs. Walter H. Reid, wife of the Base Commander and Chairman of the Branch: ".... Our efforts produced 288,484 surgical dressings for the Red Cross and for the Station Hospital approximately 25,000 surgical dressings have been produced since September 1942.... At the present time our organization is using one entire barracks which has been done over for the use of WAC personnel but was never used by them. The upstairs is given over to an office and the tables and chairs which the ladies use in their work...in addition to that a mess hall has been constructed behind our barracks for the exclusive use of the ladies participating in Red Cross work and for the members of the Ellington Field Ladies Club ."[7]

The Ellington Field Ladies Club was composed of officer's wives, and may have been the model for the Officer's Wives Club seen on all Air Force bases even today. The Ellington Field Ladies Club had a bridge luncheon twice a month; on the occasions when they met on base, the women helped with the surgical dressing work.

The volunteer work of the wives spawned another "first" at Ellington. In 1943, the women recognized the need for a safe place where the Red Cross workers could leave their children while they worked. They converted the entire downstairs of a barracks building for a nursery, and filled a small laundry building adjacent to the barracks with cribs for the smallest children's afternoon naps. The Red Cross hired four women trained in nursery work to supervise the below school-age children. In addition to supplying the cots and cribs, the volunteers gathered numerous toys, playthings, and outdoor play equipment. Mrs. Reid explained: "These arrangements make it very convenient for the Red Cross ladies to come to the field and do their work. They can be upstairs going about their duties while their children are in competent hands no further away than downstairs. I believe this is the first nursery ever opened on a post."[8] About 75 children could be accommodated at one time, but the number averaged from three to fifty on any single day. Hot lunches were available for $.20 each, and the day care service cost $.25 a day for officer's wives and $.15 a day for non-commissioned officer's wives.[9]

The wives at Ellington Field served in two other important ways. They maintained a "Spotters File," which listed the addresses of the wives and families of the officers and enlisted men stationed at the base. In case of an emergency or disaster, the file would be consulted to locate and notify the next of kin. The military wives' organizations located jobs and adequate living quarters for the cadet wives during their stay in Houston. Since general housing was not available on base, most of the cadet wives had to live some distance away and visit their husbands occasionally. Relatively few could relocate for the period of their husbands' training.

Many other Houston area women, often those who had sons, brothers or other relatives in the military, worked through the USO to help find lodging for wives and children of the men who had been sent to Ellington Field. Houstonian Glory Morris was the head of the USO during World War II.[10] Houston had several clubs and canteens that catered to the servicemen.

The rapid expansion of Ellington in the early days of 1942 necessitated an increase in the number of civilians employed in the Post Engineers office, the Post Headquarters, and the Sub-Depot. A sub-depot is an attached unit on a flying field that is not involved in any way with the flight training, and that reports directly to the commanding officer. The Sub-Depot was the unit responsible for furnishing technical supplies peculiar to flying, and for maintaining the aircraft. An article in the *Houston Chronicle* announced that "Ellington Field wants 178 men and women who must be skilled in work ranging from aircraft mechanics to leather and canvas craft."[11] Women who applied for the training had to have six months of experience in some type of work related to the training coursework. According to civil service employee Alexine Watts, Major Greig did most of the hiring. She recalled: "The training program of the Sub-Depot during 1941 and 1942 was a matter of schools. We conducted schools that ran for three months and prepared the people to do certain jobs. Major Greig had me interview the applicants. He originated the term 'Plane Janes' for our women mechanics. After an interview the person was sent to one of our schools. While they were in training they were on our apprentice rating. After completing their training they were then on a full Civil Service rating and subject to promotion."[12]

Within a month, twelve women had been selected by the federal civil service employment agency to begin training at Taylor Vocational School in Houston as mechanic helpers. They were given a 30 day course of instruction, two as instrument specialists, four as sheet metal workers, two as welders, and four as electricians.[13] Minta Allison was the first woman mechanic employed at Ellington. She owned her own watch repair shop, so Major Greig hired her and retrained her to adjust and maintain the delicate aircraft instruments.[14] In an interview, Miss Allison admitted her instrument repair work was usually a man's job. "Suits me fine, though," she said, "and I want to be where I'll be serving my country best."[15] She also reported that although she was the only woman in her department, she was treated very kindly by the men who worked there. Her supervisor worked closely with her and taught her how to remove, install, test and calibrate the instruments. She and her supervisor, Ansel Brown, had been working together about seven months when he asked her to marry him. Later, the couple was transferred to a base in DeRidder, Louisiana, where Ansel was put in charge of the instruments department. Minta's job ended when she was six or seven months pregnant. She reflected, "I had mixed feelings. I was excited about the prospect of having a baby but since the war wasn't over I didn't feel ready to quit. My son was born June 27, 1944."[16] Miss Delilah McNeill spent four years working at an auto repair shop and found that airplane motor repair work was nothing new for her. Mrs. Margaret Myers was working in a toy factory before she transitioned to making and repairing wooden airplane parts. [17] Women mechanics like Miss Clora Ellen Paulk, Mrs. Katherine R. Grahn, and Mrs. Mary Priest, went to work on the maintenance line and some were capable of completely overhauling an airplane engine. As fast as the women were trained, the Base Commander assigned

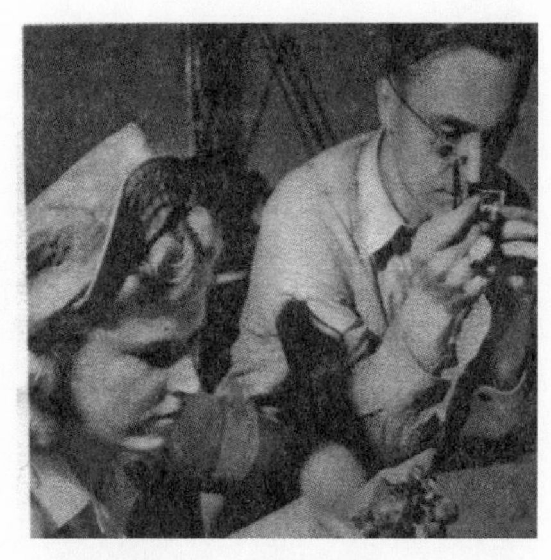

Minta Allison at work, courtesy of Minta Allison Staudenmeyer

them to various maintenance jobs. By the end of the year, more than one hundred were employed as mechanics.[18]

Plane Janes at Ellington Field, Courtesy of Minta Allison Staudenmeyer. L to R. Delilah McNeil, Mrs. Mary F. Priest, Clora E. Paulk, Mrs. Katherine Grahn

Msgt. Wilbur Lage, in charge of the parachutes and fabric department at Ellington Field, and a twenty year veteran of the Army.[19] "If you really want to know", he said, leaning forward with a confidential air, "these girls are as competent as any soldiers I've ever seen on the job. At sewing, they beat the men all hollow."

Three other Houston women were put to work in the parachutes department. Mrs. Inez Kirkpatrick, who had worked for an awning manufacturer, Mrs. Marguerite Todd, and Mrs. Katherine Peck used their sewing skills to repair parachutes. It was a painstaking job that allowed for no errors. Eventually, they were also entrusted with the highly skilled job of packing parachutes. Every sixty days, all the parachutes were unrolled, checked, repaired if necessary, and repacked. The repacking took about an hour per parachute, and was usually only done by someone with years of experience, since the aviator's lives depended on each parachute being perfectly in order.

The women proved themselves equal to the task. Five minutes later, Mrs. Kirkpatrick was saying in an equally confident manner, "You know, sergeants are supposed to be as hard as nails, but Sergeant Lage is an awfully nice man, pleasant and helpful."[20]

WFTD and WASP—The Women Who Flew

In 1942, the Army Air Corps created two units to train women pilots; the Women's Auxiliary Ferrying Squadron (WAFS), organized by Nancy Love, on September 10, 1942, and the Women's Flight Training Detachment (WFTD), organized by Jacqueline Cochran, on September 15, 1942. Nancy Love (1914-1976) was an early pioneer in the development of student flying clubs in U. S. colleges and a charter member of the Ninety-Nines, a female pilots' organization founded by Amelia Earhart (1897-1937). She succeeded in convincing the head of the Army Air Corps Ferrying Division's Domestic Wing that the idea of using experienced women pilots to supplement the existing pilot force was a good one. Jacqueline Cochran (1906-1980) America's most famous woman pilot and the first woman to fly a bomber across the Atlantic, had campaigned for civilian women pilots to be recruited into the Army Air Service and used in non-combat roles to free up male pilots for combat duty. The WAFs and WFTDs were merged on June 28, 1943, to form the Women's Airforce Service Pilots (WASP). [21] The WFTD and WASP women pilots trained at Aviation Enterprises at the Houston Airport, and later at Avenger Field in Sweetwater, Texas, with occasional support like the loan of equipment or personnel from Ellington Field. The Ellington Field Camp Surgeon's Report for 1943 mentioned that it was necessary to loan a medical officer to the Women's Flying Training Detachment (WFTD) at Houston Airport from January to June of 1943, until the transfer of the unit to Avenger Field relieved Ellington Field of this duty.[22]

There are entire books written about the experiences of these women pilots, but a few notes will be included here to remind modern readers what these pioneering women endured to become the first class of women military pilots. It was rumored at the time that the War Department had sent a letter to the commanding officer of the training field in Houston. The letter supposedly said the War Department did not think the women would ever be able to fly military aircraft, and to get rid of them. Geri Lamphere, one of the women in the first class (43-W-1) who had earned her private and commercial pilots licenses and a flying instructor's rating before coming to the school, described the lack of care given to the women:

> At Aviation Enterprises there was no place for us to eat or go to the bathroom. We had to go up to the terminal, which was about half a mile from where we trained. We were so cold in January…we did complain so much they brought over a box of castoffs (uniforms, ed.) from Ellington Field. Not a suit was under size 44 and the smallest shoe was size eleven. If we put on the boots, we couldn't feel the rudder, and (it was so cold) if we didn't have them on we couldn't feel it either… We all wondered what …was going on at the fence between Ellington and our field. They had a lot of heavy equipment cutting a big hole in the fence. Then they shoved these planes through to our field. We just couldn't understand why they didn't fly them over from next door…they had decided to junk those planes when they found out they had termites in the wings. Then the commanding officer over there said to send them over to the girls as they wouldn't be there long, anyway…I was horrified…[23]

On April 24, 194, the first 23 women of the WASP received their Silver Wings and Army diplomas as pilots with the 319th Flying Training Detachment, Civilian Ferry pilots, at Ellington Field. The next two classes, designated 43-2 and 43-3, were in attendance. Eventually, each woman pilot became qualified to fly, some qualified in as many as nineteen types of military aircraft,[24] even the notorious B-26 Marauder bomber. Marjorie Sanford Thompson recalled the way the women of class 43-W-5 got to fly the B-26;

> Upon completion of my training in Sweetwater, I was sent to Love Field in Dallas. I was there only three weeks and had not had the opportunity to ferry one aircraft when I was sent to Dodge City, Kansas to be trained to fly the B-26 Marauder. Four of the bombers had crashed the previous month killing the entire crews and the instructors reported that the students no longer wanted to fly the plane…Jacqueline Cochran and General "Hap" Arnold decided that if girls would fly it, the men would no longer be afraid of it. The commanding officer at Dodge City told us that it was a morale booster…we were taken to the Adjutant's office where plaster casts were made of our teeth for any needed identification in the future….[25]

> *Frankly, I didn't know in 1941 if a slip of a young girl could fight the controls of a B-17 in the heavy weather they would naturally encounter in operational flying. Those of us who had been flying for twenty or thirty years knew that flying an airplane was something you do not learn overnight.... Well, now in 1944...we can only come to one conclusion- the entire operation has been a success. It is on record that women can fly as well as men. Certainly we haven't been able to build an airplane that you can't handle.... So, on this last graduation day, I salute you and all WASPS. We of the AAF(Army Air Force) are proud of you; we will never forget our debt to you.*[26]
>
> Gen. H.H. Arnold, WASP Graduation Speech, Avenger Field, Sweetwater Texas, Dec. 7, 1944.[27]

The WASP was disbanded in 1944, but despite filling their role admirably and logging thousands of flight hours serving their country, the women were not given full military status and benefits until 1977.

WACS

Capt. Louise E. Bain 1st Lt. Helen W. Boyd 2nd Lt. Emily E. Sewell

From Army Air Force Training Command Yearbook

On June 7, 1943, the Army activated the 788th Women's Army Auxiliary Corps (WAAC) Post Headquarters Company, comprised of eighteen enlisted women and two women officers,[28] at Ellington Field to fill a wide variety of jobs in the duty roster and relieve male soldiers for combat duty. The WAAC's housing included: an Officer's Quarters, Orderly Room, Supply Room, Day Room, a site for a proposed Hairdressing Shop, two two-story barracks, and a separate Mess Hall.[29]

On August 13th, 1943, Congress passed a bill authorizing the formation of the Women's Army Corps. The next day, all the women of the 788th WAAC Post at Ellington Field who wanted to become part of the regular Army as a member of the Women's Army Corps were sworn in during a mass ceremony. Capt. Louise Bain, herself a graduate of the first WAACS officer Candidate School at Fort Des Moines, Iowa in 1942,[30] proudly marched her women soldiers to a position immediately in front of the reviewing stand where the Post Personnel Officer administered The Oath of Enlistment. The rest of the base, from commanding Officer Col. Walter Reid to the lowliest private, stood at attention while the women took the oath. As an additional tribute, squadrons of airplanes passed overhead in close formation. At the end of the ceremony, every squadron of men passed in a Full Garrison Review before the women, who were now part of the "regular" Army and no longer a semi-official auxiliary.[31] On October 19, 1943, the 788th WAAC Post was inactivated and the unit's designation was changed to the Army Air Force Women's Army Corps (AAF WAC) Detachment, Ellington Field, Texas. [32]

Initially, considerable doubt existed on post about how suitable women were for work in the Army, but the women's hard work dispelled any reservations. An acknowledgement of the hard work put in by the first group of WACs at Ellington was shown by the enormous number of requests for additional WAC personnel that came into Base Headquarters. As a tribute, on December 12, 1943, the Garrison Flag was flown in honor of the WAC Detachment on a specially designated "Salute the WAC Day."[33] In March of 1944, when sixty more women were assigned to the AAF WAC Detachment at Ellington, they were in such high demand that their assignments had to be made on a priority basis.

Newly recruited women embarked on the two-month WAC Mobilization Training Program[34] designed by WAC headquarters to familiarize them with military life and expectations. The course began with a two-hour lecture on military courtesy and customs, followed by a reading of the Articles of War and the Soldier's and Sailor's Relief Act. The women then spent two more hours learning how to properly wear and care for their uniforms, after which a clothing check made sure there were no shortages or discrepancies in their articles of clothing or insignia.

The women received the same basic training as the male recruits. They were even subjected to the twelve-hour course in Chemical Warfare, which ended with the much-dreaded demonstration of the effectiveness of the gas mask. In this demonstration, recruits were brought into a building or trailer with their gas masks in place, a tear gas bomb was set off, and the recruits were instructed to remove their gas masks. No one needed a second demonstration to prove to them that in an attack, life with a gas mask on was infinitely better than life without one. The women also received four hours of training on Malaria Control instead of the standard four-hour First Aid course because of the frequency of malaria in the nearly-tropical climate of the Houston area.

The medical staff necessarily tailored some course work for women, however. The male medical examiner presented the first hour of a Preventative Medicine course to the entire WAC Detachment that included a discussion of female anatomy, the menstrual cycle, mechanism of birth, and venereal disease. During the second hour, the female Detachment Commander, Capt. Louise E. Bain, explored the psychology and moral aspects of sexual relationships. This lecture was ordered by a confidential WAC directive sent to all WAC Detachment Commanders from the Headquarters in Washington, D.C., for the protection of the female recruits, who were mostly young, unmarried women, many far from home for the first time.

The coursework ended with a brief discussion by Capt. Bain of WAC Current Events across the country. An explanation of the organization itself and the present chain of command followed, with specific information about the disbanding of the WAC headquarters in Washington. Capt. Bain then gave recognition to WACS in key positions across the country.

WACS enthusiastically attended optional courses in French, German and typing given by the base Special Services office. WAC Pfc. Marian Finlay was selected to teach the course in French. Three WACs took Army Correspondence courses in accounting, bookkeeping and radio communications procedures. The women assigned as Radio Mechanics enrolled in an optional course in radio code offered by the Pilot Ground School.

As further proof of the women's accomplishments, members of the Detachment received fifteen Good Conduct medals during this period, and twenty members acted as a guard of honor for twenty-two female recruits sworn into the WAC to serve in the Army Air Service. WAC officers from Ellington Field shared Provost Marshal duty with the downtown Houston Recruiting Office every Saturday night as part of a coordinated effort by the Houston Provost Marshal, the Armed Forces Induction Station, and Headquarters, Ellington Field, to minimize disturbances from military personnel while out on pass to Houston. During this same period, the Base Commander for the first time assigned WAC personnel at Ellington as Control Tower operators, Airplane Engine Mechanics in the Transient Hangar, and in the Guard Squadron for duty at the front gate. During the period from June 9, 1943 to March 1944, almost every department on the field had at least one WAC serving in some capacity.[35]

In their medical duties, the WACs of the Army Nurse Corps reported to the Camp Surgeon, and worked with the Red Cross to ease the condition of the ill and injured. During 1943, none of the WACs required hospitalization or serious medical attention, so it was not necessary to set up a separate hospital ward for them. The Flight Surgeon attended to routine sick call and dental work for the women in his office before the regular day began. The women were not used on ward duty with the men.[36]

In addition to their strictly military duties, the women also supported other post functions. They were in the cast of the post musical sponsored by Special Services, led the post in the number of subscriptions to the Fourth War Loan,[37] and assisted in the Infantile Paralysis (Polio) Campaign. The women also actively recruited other women for the Women's Air Corps. In November of 1943, the Ellington Post band accompanied WACs on a recruiting drive to enlist women for the Women's Army Corps. The military band made a tour of cities in southern and eastern Texas while the orchestra stayed at home and played three times a day at the WAC recruiting Post at the corner of Main and Rusk Streets in Houston. The WAC recruiting tour continued through December, then came back to the base for the holidays. A steady and successful recruiting program continued to increase the numbers of women serving in the Army. Recruiters relied on the participation of WAC units from Ellington Field in community programs, parades, and ceremonies to stir enthusiasm, and their recruiting efforts were very much enhanced by the presence of a military band. During the period from November 1, 1943 until Mar 1, 1944, WACs helped recruit 154 women for service in the Women's Army Corps at Ellington Field.

Like all other military personnel, WACs were also subject to transfers. General Order 14, dated Mar 1, 1944, directed a reorganization of Ellington Field. One of the changes under this order called for the AAF WAC Detachment to be discontinued, [38] and transferred eighteen members of the Army Nurse Corps out of Ellington. WACs were back on the base again in 1945. On June 6, 1945, fifteen WACs arrived from San Antonio Aviation Cadet Center to continue their medical and dental training at Ellington and became part of Squadron D of the 2517th Base Unit. There was also a WAC Recruiting Office on the base, as evidenced by a memorandum from the Production Line Maintenance Officer to the Historical Editor dated July 3, 1945, recording that the WAC Recruiting Office vehicles were part of the backlog of 346 Air Corps vehicles that were overloading the understaffed Automotive Maintenance Department.[39]

The incentives for young black women to join the military were the same as they were for the men—steady pay and benefits, the chance to serve their country, and the sense of self-respect wearing a uniform brought. The opportunity to travel probably stirred a few wandering hearts, as well. Margery Lewis, nee Lowery, was a young black woman living in the town of Navasota, just northwest of Houston, Texas, during World War II. Day after day she watched the airplanes from Ellington and the other airfields around Houston fly overhead. She saw the young men in her neighborhood appear at church in their crisp new uniforms and then get sent off for training and disappear into the Army.

Margery desperately wanted to serve her country, too, and she wanted to fly airplanes. It never occurred to her that her dream of being in the military might not be as possible for a young black woman as it might be for a young black man, or that becoming a pilot was not very likely for any young black person, male or female. She watched with envy as one of her girlfriends came home to visit in a WAC uniform early in the war. Margery's enthusiasm for flying diminished over the following months however, as the reports of plane crashes appeared in the local papers, and her inclination to become an army nurse disappeared when she discovered she could not stand the sight of blood. By the time she was out of school and old enough to enlist, she had decided to remain a civilian. [40]

As far as the records show, there were no black women among the

WACS stationed at Ellington Field during World War II. There are none in evidence in the photographs of the 788th Women's Army Corps or in the nurses of the medical detachment.[41] However, by 1950, there were black women shown in the 3500th WAF Squadron, and on the Ellington WAF Softball Team.[42] There were also many black men and women who worked as civilians from World War II to 2005 at Ellington, as documented in many subsequent squadron histories.

WAC Softball Team, Ellington Air Force Base from Navigation School Yearbook, 1950 Ellington Air Force Base

The creation of the Air force as a separate branch of the military in 1948 meant Ellington Field was now Ellington Air Force Base and all of the women stationed there were no longer designated as WACs, but WAFs—Women's Air Force, which was a separate corps under the auspices of the Air Force.[43] Women gradually became completely integrated into the Air Force instead of a separate division. In 1973, the Air Force announced that the 25th anniversary of the Women's Air Force held on June 12th would be the last official observance, since women were now an official part of the regular Air Force. The numbers of women in the Air Force increased from 1,500 in 1948 to 18,000 in 1973. By 1973, women were able to compete equally for promotions in the enlisted and officer ranks, and were trained, assigned and administered under essentially the same policies and procedures. The only career fields not open to women at that time were direct combat specialties, which were restricted as male only duties by law. Almost one-fourth of the women serving in the Air Force were stationed overseas, and about one fourth of women were married. In 1973, there were five female officers serving at Ellington Air Force Base.[44]

WACs, from A Camera Trip through Ellington Field

Change of Command

In an interview at the end of 1943, Col. Reid voiced his opinion about the important work that had been accomplished at Ellington during his tenure as Commanding Officer:

> Lt. Havins, Ellington Field Historical Officer asked: *'What do you consider the outstanding accomplishment of this station'? Col. Reid answered: 'The training of some 15,000 enlisted men and securing the services of about 250 officer instructors. Of course we have also trained a lot of pilots, too.'*[45]

On April 10, 1944, Col. Walter H. Reid was reassigned to temporary duty to San Angelo, Texas, as acting wing commander of the Thirty-fourth Flying Training Wing.[46] His subsequent permanent assignment in

May of 1944 was to the advanced navigation school at Selman Field, Louisiana. In September of 1945, he was transferred to Randolph Field, Texas to be the Commanding Officer.[47] In June of 1946, Col. Walter Reid was awarded the Army's Legion of Merit for "Outstanding Organizational Ability" for his work at Ellington Field. A newspaper article pointed out that "...under Colonel Reid's able leadership, Ellington Field rose to the height of efficiency and produced a flow of pilots, bombardiers and navigators urgently needed for the successful prosecution of the war."[48] (See Biography Section) Col. Ralph C. Rockwood assumed temporary command of Ellington Field on April 10, 1944, due to the reassignment of Col. Walter H. Reid, and full command of Ellington on May 29, 1944. On March 15, 1946, the base was again deactivated under the Air Defense Command, and later that same year placed under the jurisdiction of the 10th Air Force.[49] The base did not remain on inactive status very long until it was needed again. In 1947, Ellington Field became a full-fledged base again, as part of a brand new branch of the service.

End Notes

[1] *Ellington 1918* (Houston: Private printing, 1918), p.106, lists the women; Mrs. Wm. McDonald, Director Hostess, Mrs. H.A. Campbell, Assistant Hostess, Miss Sarah E. Quinn, Cafeteria Director Hostess, and Mrs. Frank A. Burroughs, Business Hostess.

[2] The influenza pandemic of 1917-1918 killed more people in one year than the Bubonic Plague, the infamous "Black Death", did in its four year reign of terror. This unusual flu was most deadly to people ages 20-40. Of the U.S. soldiers who died in the war in Europe, half of them were killed by the flu, and not the enemy. An estimated 43,000 servicemen mobilized for WWI died of influenza. Worldwide, the pandemic claimed between 20 and 40 million lives, and has been called the most devastating epidemic in recorded world history. Molly Billings, *The Influenza Pandemic of 1918*, Stanford University Education Group, at www.stanford.edu/group/virus/uda.

[3] Ibid. p. 107

[4] Ibid, p. 219, lists head Nurse, Amelia J. Valentine, OH; Nurses, Georgia I. Brady, TX; R. Mora Clark, TX; Mary Anne Collins, KS; Margaret V. Elkins, TX; Jennie Honaker, Nellie Honaker, MO; Mary Linder, NY; Bess Meador, TX; and Mahala S. Rice, MI.

[5] Robert A. Wilkins, interview by Lt. T.R. Havins, in *The History of Ellington Field, 1941-1944* (Maxwell AFB: AFHRA, 2002), Microfilm, roll B2175.

[6] Col. Walter H. Reid, letter to the wives of all Officers and Non-Commissioned Officers, dated May 6, 1943.

[7] Mrs. Walter H. Reid. Interview by Lt. T.R. Havins, in *The History of Ellington Field, 1941-1944* (Maxwell AFB: AFHRA, 2002), Microfilm, roll B2175, pp. 1, 2.

[8] Ibid., p. 2.

[9] Col. Reid letter to the wives.

[10] Marguerite Johnston, *Houston, the Unknown City, 1836-1946* (College Station: Texas A&M University Press, fourth printing, 1994), p. 358.

[11] Houston Chronicle, February 8, 1942.

[12] Alexine G. Watts, interview by Lt.T.R.Havins, in *The History of Ellington Field 1941-1944* (Maxwell AFB: AFHRA, 2002) Microfilm, roll B2175, p. 70.

[13] "12 Houston Women To Start Training For Defense Jobs", *Houston Press...1942*

[14] Interview, Mrs. Minta Staudenmayer, by author, April 14, 2005 by telephone.

[15] "Ellington Women's Nimble Fingers Tighten Noose Around Neck of Hitler & Company", *Houston Press,* ...1942.

[16] Minta Allison Staudenmayer, interview by author, Houston, May 10, 2005.

[17] "Women Mechanics Help to Keep "Em Flying at Ellington field", *Houston...May 17, 1942.*

[18] Alexine G. Watts, interview by Lt.T.R.Havins, in *The History of Ellington Field 1941-1944* (Maxwell AFB: AFHRA, 2002) Microfilm, roll B2175, p. 71.

[19] "Ellington Women's Nimble Fingers Tighten Noose Around Neck of Hitler & Company", *Houston Press...1942.*

[20] Ibid.

[21] "The Women Pilots of WW II", article on website at www.wasp-wwii.org. [Accessed 2/1/03].

[22] Camp Surgeon's Report, 1943. *The History of Ellington Field 1941-1944*. (Maxwell AFB: AFHRA, 2002) Microfilm roll B2175.

[23] Celeste Graves, *A View From The Doghouse of the 319th AAFWTD.* (Bloomington: AuthorHouse, 2004) 38, 39.

[24] Ibid. 84, 85.

[25] Ibid. 226.

[26] Anne Noggle, *For God, Country, and the Thrill of It: Women Airforce Service Pilots in World War II* (College Station: Texas A&M University Press, 1990), p. 13.

[27] For a roster of Class 43-1 members, see Appendix 1.

[28] The original officers were Margaret K. Kelley, 2nd officer (WAAC CO.O) and Helen W. Boyd, 3rd officer (WAAC mess and Supply Officer). They signed in at Post Headquarters June 11,1943.

[29] Louise E. Bain, *History of the AAF WAC Detachment, Ellington Field Texas, 9 June 1943—1 March 1944, Former Designations and Assignments. 788th WAAC Post Headquarters Company, 7 June 1943—19 October 1943* (Maxwell AFB: AFRHA, 2002) Microfilm, roll B 2175.

[30] "Graduates of the First WAACS OCS at Fort Des Moines, Iowa, 29 August, First Company", Fort Des Moines wesbite at www.fortdesmoines.org/female. [Accessed 4/4/03].

[31] For a listing of the women in the 788th Women's Army Corps in 1943, see Appendix 2.

[32] Bain, p. 2.

[33] Ibid., p. 4.

[34] Ibid., pp. 3-6.

[35] Ibid., p. 3.

[36] " Camp Surgeon's Report," 1943, Microfilm, roll B2175, p. 14.

[37] The Fourth War Loan War Bond Drive began on January 18, 1944, and ended February 15, 1944. The drive sold almost 70 million separate E bonds, worth $16.7 billion. Targeted buyers were farmers and women. "Brief History of World War Two Advertising Campaigns. War Loans, Bonds. " John W. Hartman Center for Sales and Marketing Advertising websitewww.lib.duke.edu/adaccess. Accessed 2/24/2004.

[38] *History of the 2517th Base Unit* (Maxwell AFB: AFHRA, 2002) Microfilm, roll B2175, p. 5.

[39] Ibid., p. 75.

[40] Margery Lewis interview by author,.at her place of work, May 10, 2005.

[41] *Army Air Forces Training Command, Ellington Field, Texas* (Baton Rouge: Army and Navy Publishing Company of Louisiana, c.1942), 42,43, 184, 185.

[42] *Navigation School, Ellington Air Force Base 1950.* (Baton Rouge: A&N Pictorial Publishers, 1950).

[43] *Ellington Air Force Base Aircraft Observer Training, (*Baton Rouge: Army & Navy Publishing Company, Inc., 1956, 50.

[44] *The Skylander,* June 8, 1973, p. 11.

[45] Reid, Microfilm, roll B2175.

[46] *The Houston Post,* November 25, 1953.

[47] *The Houston Post, June 30, 1946.*

[48] Ibid.

[49] *Historical Background—Ellington Air Force Base, Houston, Texas,"* no author, paper supplied by the Houston Airport System Operations Office, Ellington Field, p. 3.

CHAPTER V

Ellington Air Force Base, 1947-1976

The National Security Act of 1947 created the United States Air Force as a separate branch of the Armed Forces. On September 26, 1947, the Secretary of Defense ordered the personnel of the Army Air Forces (AAF) transferred from the Department of the Army to the Department of the Air Force and established as the United States Air Force (USAF). [1] Ellington Field became Ellington Air Force Base.

In 1948, Ellington Air Force Base operated on a limited basis as an Air Force Reserve and Texas National Guard base. In April of 1949, the United States Air Force Air Training Command activated the 3605th Base Observer-Training program at Ellington Air Force Base, with Colonel Benjamin T. Starkey as Base Commander, as the only post-war navigation school in the nation. The initial goal of the school was to retrain World War II veteran navigator/bombardiers in the latest air navigation techniques and familiarize them with the new, long-range bomber aircraft. A second, longer course gave full training in navigation to new aviation cadets. The refresher course emphasized navigating by modern radar in bad weather and over polar areas where ordinary compasses and maps had been useless in the past. Flying over the North Pole became increasingly important as Russia built up its arsenal of Intercontinental Ballistic Missiles (ICBMs). The polar route was the shortest, fastest route to Russia. The base was expanded to house up to 2,000 personnel and handle the take-offs and landings of about 125 aircraft. At its peak, the navigation school graduated as many as 1,500 students a year at Ellington. The rebirth of Ellington Field caused much excitement in Houston, because along with the 2,000 to 3,000 permanent military personnel, the new program brought civilian jobs and a payroll of more than $1 million dollars, most of which would be spent locally.

The Early Cold War Years

The wartime draft instituted by the newly formed Selective Service System in 1940 was expanded in 1941, and expired in 1947. Beginning in 1946, the United State's rivalry with the Soviet Union and subsequent worldwide fight against communism spawned more than four decades of continuous mobilization, or state of military readiness-the longest in U.S. history. In 1948, the communists overtook Czechoslovakia in a major military coup and blockaded Berlin, driving the U.S. to once again prepare for war and reinstate the draft.[2] In the 1950's, North Korea attacked South Korea. the Red Chinese invaded mainland China, the United States began fighting a war in North Korea, and The Russians had ballistic missiles pointed toward the U.S. The threat of spreading communist aggression was taken very seriously.[3] The exploits of military leaders like Generals Dwight D. Eisenhower and Douglas MacArthur made the headlines of the *Houston Chronicle* and *The Houston Post* on a weekly basis alongside a roster of those Texas men killed or missing in action in Korea. The United States Department of Defense military mobilization plan called for 3,500,000 men to go into the armed forces.[4]

When the Korean War broke out, all of Ellington Air Force Base's seven reserve units were called to active duty. Col. William L. Lee assumed command of the 3605th Navigation Training Wing March 1, 1950. The total number of students who passed through the courses at Ellington for the period of 1950-1956 was 18,836. During the same period, these students logged 424,431 hours of flying time, and covered millions of air miles. The number of miles flown during 1953 is representative of the period. In 1953 alone, pilots and student pilots flew 5,490,376 air miles-the equivalent of twenty three trips to the moon.[5]

3605TH Navigation Training Wing

In April of 1950, when the 3605th Navigator Training Wing was reactivated at Ellington Air Force Base, it had the distinction of being the first and only navigator training school in the Air Force. The use of large transport planes and heavy bombers to fly missions for the Air Force all around the world required that each flight crew member be a specialist in his own field. Consequently, the pilots, bombardiers, radio and radar operators, gunners and photographers in the crew looked to the navigators to always keep track of where they were, when they would arrive at their destination, and which compass heading they should fly to get there. The primary mission of the training was to teach airplane crew members the latest aviation technology available to keep the airplanes on course and on time. Following graduation, the training cadets were commissioned second lieutenants in the United States Air Force Reserve with aeronautical ratings as navigators.[6]

Marching at EllingtonField rom A Camera Trip Through Ellington Field

The training aircraft was a specially adapted, twin-engine Convair T-29, developed by the Air Force and built by Consolidated-Vultee Aircraft Corporation. It was commonly referred to as the "flying classroom," because it was equipped with fourteen stations for student navigators. Each station had a loran scope, radio compass, altimeter, air speed indicator, drift meter, and map table. Four instructors, many with combat experience, accompanied each flight, permitting on-the-spot observation and training during actual flights.[7] The Convairs were equipped with the most up-to-date electronic equipment and air navigation instruments.[8] The 42-week course provided highly specialized training required by the complex engineering that allowed the planes to fly at the speed of sound. During the course of study, the students spent 270 hours on the theory and practice of electronics and 250 hours on navigation. At the end of the course, students were qualified as radar operators and radar navigators, proficient in dead reckoning, radio, LORAN (Long Distance Radar Navigation) and celestial navigation. The United States House of Representatives approved a bill for $4,787,000 to expand the training facilities at Ellington. The first class of the observer-training group graduated in April 1952.[9] Colonel Merlin I. Carter followed Colonel Lee as commander of the wing in August, 1952, and was himself followed by Colonel Norman Callish, who served from July, 1953. to August, 1958. During his command, the Wing was redesignated as the 3605th Aircraft Observer Training Wing.

The 3605th Air Base Group handled the administrative and "housekeeping" duties of the base. The Group was made up of five separate squadrons of officers, airmen and WAFS who worked in administrative, maintenance, and support positions such as, office workers, carpenters, military police, mechanics, firemen and cooks. These were the men and women who kept the base running smoothly day-to-day.The five squadrons were Support, Air Police, Motor Vehicle, Food Service, WAF, and the 722nd Air Force Band. For instance the job of feeding all the personnel on base was handled by the 3605th Food Services Squadron. The nutrition and care of the airmen was the top priority of the Food Service, and the Food Services Squadron was in charge of four huge dining halls.[10]

Other units on base included the 722nd Air Force Band, under the direction of Chief Warrant Officer Harold E. Waite, the 3500th W.A.F Squadron, under the command of 1st Lieutenant Ellen Thomas Gilbert, a Weather Department, the 1923-3 AACS Detachment, under the command of Captain Charles E. Nash, and the 3607th Military Training Squadron (Flying Support), Major Richard D. Goree, Commanding Officer.

The Impact of Militarization and Mobilization

As the United States responded to the surprise attack against South Korea and the possibility of a Soviet invasion of Western Europe, a new national security policy (NSC #68) was put in place. Paul Nitze, a principal proponent of NSC #68, warned "Our military strength is becoming dangerously inadequate… Budgetary considerations will need to be subordinated to the stark fact that our very independence as a nation may be at stake." Between 1950 and 1952, U.S. defense spending soared from $13 billion to more than $60 billion annually. Military readiness touched all aspects of American society and culture.[11]

The citizens of Houston, Texas, wove threads of militarization into their daily lives. The Women's section of the *Houston Chronicle* began to include recipes for treats that would survive being shipped to the boys overseas. Newspaper article titles revealed the concern and conflict women felt about the possibility of women being drafted into the military or needed in the war plants. [12] An article written by Josephine Lowman, entitled "Work Hard, But Keep Your Lipstick On" counseled women with the following advice:

> This is a very difficult time for peace loving peoples everywhere. The war just past left a scar which is still tender. We girded ourselves to meet the last emergency, and now the necessity of facing another such experience is like pulling off the scab before the wound is entirely healed. We can pray and hope and work to avoid war but we are in peril and if any of the fair sex is still hiding heads in the sand it had better wake up and face reality. Had we women done so sooner and insisted on universal military training some time ago today's mess would probably be less drastic…This is not a time for luxuries and self-indulgence, but it is a time when good grooming, physical health, vitality, and a calm personality are true benefits. Let us think clearly and put our shoulders to the wheel, but let us keep our lipstick on.[13]

Women had gained valuable military and defense experience in the services during World War II, and by 1950, they were an established presence in the military. In February, 1951, the Women's Army Corps (WAC) Veterans Association announced that it was going to ask more than 1,000 of its members to enlist in the nation's civil defense program. [14] By 1951, there were more than 25,000 women serving in the Army (WAC), Navy (WAVES), Air Force (WAF) and Marine Corps (WM)[15] all across the country. Lt. Stella Baker was a member of Jacqueline Cochran's WASPS during World War II, and she was recalled to service in February of 1951. She was stationed at Ellington Air Force Base, and assigned to the Comptroller's Office. She was the first WAF officer to be married at one of Ellington's four chapels when she married Clarence G. Claiborne on October 23, 1951 in Chapel No. 1.[16]

"Shooting the Sun" with a sextant, from Ellington Air Force Base Navigation School Yearbook, 1950

Universities, colleges and civilian organizations began militarizing. The University of Houston and Rice University started up its Reserve Officer Training programs (ROTC) and began coordinating Civil Defense programs with the local communities. At a Civil Defense Rally sponsored by the American Legion and the University of Houston, Col. K. K. Black, commander of the 158th Aircraft Warning and Control Group at Ellington Field, warned the several hundred Houstonians present, " The prime target of enemy bombers in the event the United States is forced into a third World War will not be in the big Eastern cities, but the second largest port city in the nation-Houston. Why knock out Detroit, Chicago, or New York and its large assembly plants of tanks when you can knock out the gas that runs those tanks? And it's high time Washington realized this is the nations' number one strategic area."[17]

In January of 1951, the Air Force announced it would call 150,000 National Guard and Air Force Reservists to active duty nationwide, which affected the 60,000 volunteer reserve airmen and 20,000 volunteer reserve officers registered in the Houston and Harris County area. Neither Col. William L. Lee, commander of Ellington Air Force Base, nor Col. Black was told which units would be recalled immediately, or how many additional men would be assigned to the base.[18] At the time, Ellington had approximately 1,000 officers, 2,600 enlisted men, 300 aviation cadets and 800 civilian workers already, but there were some empty barracks that could be reopened and used to house the new personnel if necessary. By January 20, the Department of Defense announced that an additional 1,150 people would be assigned to the air base. [19]

Lt. Col. Charles M. McDermott, the base executive officer, began working on the organizational details of the base expansion immediately.[20] Three days later, Col. Lee announced that all of Ellington's seven organized reserve units had been called up to active duty. The reservists had a mandatory three-day tour of duty to receive physical examinations and to have their military records checked and brought up to date. The reservists then had a maximum of 30 days to close out their personal and business affairs before reporting to their units. However, Col. Lee warned the men not to be too hasty about terminating their personal affairs, because any of the men who failed the physical would not be recalled.[21]

Many of these reservists had been taking time away from their jobs and families to participate in local defense programs and reserve training since the end of World War II. The sudden call-up and lack of information about when and how long they would serve created chaos in their lives. Some men lost their jobs. Commissions and promotions went to other men whose futures were more settled. For many, their Air Force assignment was lower paying than the job they lost. Business owners faced being away from their businesses for an indefinite period of time. Col. Black, mentioned above, lost his business[22] because he simply was not around to manage it, and other businessmen faced similar worries when they were called up to active duty. Insurance agent and Air Reserve officer Lt. Col. Joe S. Peck was assigned as the commanding officer of the 3605th Military Training Squadron. He had served as a pilot with the Eighth Air Force in Europe in World War II. Lt. Col. Percy B. Follis, the owner of Audio Visual Aids Company, was assigned as the assistant executive officr of the 3605th Navigation Training Wing. Col. Follis served as a combat intelligence officer in Italy. Lt. Col. Dorwin C. Wright became the executive officer of the Air Base Group. He served in the China-Burma-India theater during World War II. All three reservists had been training as mobilization assignees for many months. [23]

Coastal Defense

Since the installation of the first radar system at Ellington Field in 1941, radar technology had become a major tool in defending the United States against an attack by enemy airplanes or missiles. In the spring of 1950, a new Tactical Radar Control Center was built at the La Porte, Texas, Municipal Airfield. The Control Center was operated by three units of the Texas Air National Guard; the 158th and 134th Aircraft Control Units, and the 108th Radar Calibration Detachment, which were stationed at Ellington Air Force Base as part of the 158th Aircraft Control and Warning Group (ACWG). The Headquarters of the 158th ACWG at Ellington Air Force Base was under the command of Air Force Reserve officer Col. Kermit K. Black (1907-1983). [24] The control center provided radar warning of any impending air attack or hurricane in the area, and served as the control center for dispatching fighter planes from the F-51 squadrons of the Texas Air National Guard in Houston, Dallas, and San Antonio. Veteran combat pilots manned Houston's 111th Squadron, which was based at Ellington Field, and kept it in a constant state of battle-readiness.

The groundbreaking ceremony for the Tactical Radar Control Center at the LaPorte Municipal Airport was a big event. Numerous military and civic leaders attended and took part. Mr. L.E. Posey was the Master of Ceremonies, Rev. Father Nelson of St. Mary's Catholic Church began the ceremony with an invocation. Mr. George H. Counts, commander of the 6th Battalion of the Texas State Guard, turned over the first spade of dirt with a new shovel donated by LaPorte Mayor H.J. Pfeiffer. The first shovel of dirt was placed in a box, and the box and shovel were saved, to be placed in the local Armory. Col. Black explained the purpose of saving the first shovel full of dirt dug, "We are placing this first spadeful of dirt in this box, to be saved as a reminder of the reason for the building. It will be a symbol to us, something down to earth that the people of Texas can understand."[25] He further stated, "It will always stand as a symbol of something to fight for—good old Texas Soil." [26]

The Air Force intended the Control Center to be "eyes in the sky" for the rich Gulf Coast oil and gas supplies in time of war, and it was the job of the 158th ACWG to provide defense for the entire Gulf Coast. Control centers from Victoria and Beaumont, Texas and all the radar sites along the Gulf Coast sent their information to the Control Center in La Porte. Col. Black emphasized, "The center is the heart of the defense of the area. It is the key point from which civilian defense agencies will get all information as to approaching enemy bombers, all alerts, brownouts and blackouts…" Liaison officers were also assigned from the navy, various ground units, and the Civil Aeronautics Administration. The center's radar, radio, telephone and teletype equipment were designed to locate any approaching aircraft. The center in LaPorte was linked to other units up and down the Gulf Coast over three states, and upon an alert form any unit, would immediately send fighter planes up to intercept the aircraft.[27]

The 158th ACWG group trained weekly at Ellington Field in preparation for its new role. When the new Control Center was completed in May of 1951, the 158th ACWG moved from Ellington Air Force Base to the Center at the La Porte Texas Municipal Airport, but continued to receive air support and training at Ellington. Lt. Col. Warren D. Ruth, Maj. L.C. Stansel, and Capt. Allan F. Lavers, military officers of the center, joined Col. Black for the dedication ceremony, accompanied by music supplied by the famous Ellington Air Force Band.[28]

On April 1, 1958, the Department of the Air Force transferred the responsibility for operating and maintaining the base from the 2517th Base Unit to the 10th Air Force and the 2578TH Air Base Group Continental Air Command (CONAC)[29]. Continental Air Command had also taken over full responsibility for the Civil Air Patrol (CAP), which was looking for a new location for its national headquarters. Since both the air base and the Air Patrol were under the auspices of CONAC, the headquarters for the Civil Air Patrol (CAP) was moved to Ellington Air Force Base, Texas, on 8 August 1959. They would remain at Ellington for the next eight years. The Civil Air Patrol headquarters was housed in a big, old, wooden building built at the height of World War II, which quickly became known throughout CAP as the "Ponderosa", a reference to the big house in the popular TV series *Bonanza.*[30] Just like the television show, the Ellington Ponderosa saw its share of celebrities and TV stars over the years. For instance, actor Jimmy Stewart was also a Brigadier General in the Air Force Reserves and was very active in recruiting plans for CAP. He and General Jimmy Doolittle, also a staunch CAP supporter, met many times over the years at the CAP National Headquarters at Ellington Air Force Base.

In 1967, the Department of the Air Force announced that the Continental Air Command was soon to be abolished. The Civil Air Patrol was transferred to the Air Training Command. At the same time, CAP had just leased an IBM 360 computer, which IBM refused to place in any environment that was not climate controlled, so CAP had to leave the big wooden building on Ellington. On the 15 of June 1967, CAP headquarters took up residence at Maxwell Air Force Base in Montgomery, Alabama.[31]

End Notes

[1] *Evolution of the Department of the Air Force,* Air Force History site at www.airforcehsitory.hq.af.mil/soi/evolution_of_the_departmen.htm

[2] *Americans at War: Society, Culture, and the Homefront,* (Macmillan Reference, USA, 2004).

[3] In August, 1949, the United States received intelligence data which indicated that the Russians had either exploded, or were about to explode, an atomic bomb. *Alaskan Air Command History* for 1949.

[4] Dr. Frederick H. Harbison, as quoted in *Houston Chronicle,* Feb. 20, 1951, Sec. A, 19.

[5] *Ellington AFB Historical Information,* Office of the Base Historian, 1. Figure for the distance to the moon is a mean distance of 238,712 miles.

[6] Public Information Office, *The Mission and Manner of Execution of Ellington Air Force Base, Houston, TX,* dated April 17, 1951, 1, 2.

[7] Ibid., 2

[8] *Ellington Air Force Base, Aircraft Observer Training,* (Army & Navy Publishing Company, Inc. Baton Rouge, LA, 1956), 6, 7.

[9] *Houston Observer,* February 6, 1952.

[10] *Mission and Manner,* 4.

[11] *Americans at War: Society, Culture, and the Homefront. Macmillan Reference, USA. 2004.*

[12] "Don't Draft Women Says Lady Lawyer," and "Women War Workers May Be Scarce," *Houston Chronicle,* January 1, 1951, Sec. B, 12.

[13] *Houston Chronicle,* January 23, 1951,Sec. C, 4.

[14] *Houston Chronicle,* February 19, 1951.Sec. A, 4.

[15] Dr. Esther B. Strong, as quoted in *Houston Chronicle,* February 21, 1951, Sec. B, 5.

[16] *The Skylander,* Friday, October 26, 1951.

[17] *Houston Chronicle.* February 23, 1951, Sec A, 4.

[18] *Houston Chronicle.* January 18, 1951, Sec A, 5.

[19] *Houston Chronicle,* January 20, 1951, 1.

[20] *Houston Chronicle,* January 20, 1951, 1.

[21] *Houston Chronicle,* Jan. 23, 1951, 2.

[22] Col. Black's letter to Senator Olin Teague, dated April 14, 1958.

[23] *Houston Chronicle,* February 25, 1951. Sec. A, 26.

[24] Col. Black was one of a fairly small group of men who had experience with radar-aided navigation. He had been put in charge of the ground force radar research at Belmar, New Jersey, where the radar equipment was developed in 1943. He assisted in running the original tests on ground control approach of airplanes by radar at Fort Dix, New Jersey. In his civilian life, he was also the President of the Navigation Instrument Company located on Clinton Drive near the Houston Ship Channel.

[25] *The Houston Post,* July 13, 1950, Sec. I, 18.

[26] *La Porte Liberal,* July 14, 1950, p. 1.

[27] *Houston Chronicle,* February 19, 1951, 19.

[28] *Official Program* for the Dedication of the Air Defense Control Center and Presentation

of Battle Honors to the 158th Aircraft Control and Warning Group May 26, 27, 1951, in the private papers of Col. K.K. Black, now in the possession of Kathryn Black Morrow, Houston, Texas.

[29] The Continental Air Command had jurisdiction over Air Force units that were concerned with the direct defense of the United States. These included the Air Defense Command, which supervised the training of the Air National Guard and the administration and training of the Air Reserve, and the fighter interceptor units of the Tactical Air Command based on the American continent. This command included the First, Fourth, Tenth and Fourteenth Air Forces. "History of U.S.A.F" in *Navigation School, Ellington Air Force Base, 1950* (Baton Rouge, A&N Pictorial Publishers, 1950), 6.

[30] Civil Air Patrol information courtesy of Col. Leonard A. Blascovich, CAP National Historian, 100-30 Elgar Place, Apt 30-H, Bronx, NY 10475-5048. E-Mail lblascovich@cap.gov.

[31] Ibid.

CHAPTER VI

The Space Program Comes to Ellington

The establishment of the Manned Spacecraft Center (MSC) in Houston, Texas, was a product of the major public policy decisions that developed subsequent to the flight of Russia's Sputnik I satellite in 1957. Russia's spectacular success with Sputnik hurt American pride deeply. The fact that Russia was the first superpower in space dramatized the lag in American scientific technology, and suggested the possibility of a gap in U.S. defenses and caused a decline in American prestige abroad. The Russian success confirmed the fear that Soviet rocket technology included intercontinental ballistic capability and presented an immediate threat to U.S. national defense. In the spring of 1961, several events occurred that led to the creation of the MSC. On April 12, 1961, Russia put the first man in space. U.S.S.R. Air Force pilot Yuri Gagarin's single orbit around the earth dealt another severe blow to America's pride. On May 25, 1961, six weeks after the Gagarin flight, President John F. Kennedy (1917-1963) announced an acceleration in the U.S. space program and called for the nation to commit itself to the goal of landing an man on the moon and returning him safely to earth before the decade was out. [1]

On September 19, 1961, the National Aeronautics and Space Administration (NASA) announced that Houston, Texas, had been selected over twenty other cities as the site of a control center for the nation's newest space program. NASA chose Houston in part because of its vast oil and petrochemical industry, Houston's ship channel and port facilities which provided an excellent means of transporting the bulky space vehicles to other NASA locations, the scientific and research facilities available at Rice

University, the close proximity of the University of Houston and the Texas Medical Center, and the presence of the Houston International Airport.[2] The Space Task Group at Langley Field, Virginia, now renamed the Manned Spacecraft Center, was on its way to the Gulf Coast. The Houston Chamber of Commerce proclaimed the announcement as the most significant single event in the city's economic history. Houston area scientists predicted that it would bring some of the most brilliant minds in the country to Houston.[3]

The move to Houston began immediately. Before the month was out, the Manned Spacecraft Center in Virginia sent an advance team to Houston to make arrangements for housing and temporary office space for the 1,700 personnel who would be arriving over the next few months. [4] Martin Byrnes and Roy Aldridge were assigned the task of locating temporary facilities that could be used until the permanent site was built. This was no easy task. The site chosen for the new center was a swampy cow pasture about twenty-three miles south of Houston, and about eight miles south of Ellington Field. There was little development in the area, and almost no housing. The advance team had to continue to manage their projects in Virginia while simultaneously moving the MSC people to Houston. Mr. Aldridge explained: "In those days everybody did everything… because we had hundreds of people on their way to Houston. We were running the Mercury program, getting the Gemini and Apollo Programs started and trying to set up the Center at the same time…[5] "

Dave W. Lang, one of the advance team members sent to procure housing and supplies for the families, vividly remembered his first impressions of the new site, "Bill Parker picked me up at the airport and we drove over to the Gulf Freeway… we drove and we drove and about all we could see was flat barren prairie. Finally I asked Bill, 'Where is Houston?' He Said, 'Well, it is 23 miles back the other way!' ….We crossed over the Freeway and drove through a little town called Webster. At that time Webster was a village of maybe 300 people, with a one-pump gas station and a little country store….We drove down a 2-lane road…off to the north there was an old decrepit windmill, a water tank, and some cows. Bill said, 'Well, there is the site', and I said 'Bill, you must be kidding. Nobody could have done this!' he said, 'No, this is where it is.'"[6]

As the men continued to tour the area, they witnessed the devastation caused by hurricane Carla a few weeks previously. Mud and debris was everywhere, and some houses had been blown completely off their foundations. The devastation was incomprehensible to a man from stately Virginia. Lang continued with his description of the sight, "Near the bridge, a 60-foot yacht was lying on its side in the mud....The ditches were full of furniture and clothes.... There weren't very many houses...and those along the waterfront in these areas had been severely damaged by Hurricane Carla.... I thought to myself, 'How...am I supposed to bring my wife down here?" At the time we lived in the beautiful rolling hills of the Miami Valley in Ohio and now I planned to bring her down to this flat Gulf Coast prairie. That was going to a real experience, I felt sure."[7]

Under such circumstances, mundane matters like getting from one office to another, phoning a colleague, or even finding a desk was complicated, but these obstacles scarcely slowed the pace of the program. The team negotiated leases for fourteen office buildings scattered all over south Houston, and worked out a Joint Use Agreement with the Continental Air Command for hangar space and runway use at Ellington Field.[8] The MSC team broke ground at the 1,620 acre site in March of 1962, and began construction of the permanent facilities. As the first buildings were completed in September of 1963, the Center began to move all MSC personnel out of the buildings they had been occupying across south Houston, and by June of 1964, MSC had moved all its offices either to the new MSC facility in Clear Lake, or to nearby Ellington Air Force Base.[9]

Ellington Air Force Base was the largest location available to MSC procurement team. Some of the World War II era wooden barracks were occupied by the Air Force Reserve and other agencies, but many were available for immediate occupancy. Most of the buildings were in need of rehabilitation since they had been empty for fifteen to twenty years, but they were easily converted into office space. The water systems and electrical wiring were old and the buildings were not air- conditioned. The wooden floors showed signs of major rotting, and would need to be re-timbered to bear the load of file cabinets, lab, and printing equipment. Initially, the MSC team anticipated it would only be housed at Ellington for one or two years. Martin Byrnes, Manager of the Center Operations Office, and the Project Director Robert Gilruth debated how much money the Center should spend on repairing and adapting temporary space. Director Gilruth was also very concerned that the impression the shoddy temporary headquarters made would hamper attracting high quality aerospace talent into the program.[10] Dave Lang also had memories of the buildings at Ellington, "Even after we remodeled those barracks at Ellington Field into offices, when the days were warm the bugs would come out of the walls. Also one unhappy aspect of a barracks; after 17 years as a BOQ (Bachelor Officer's Quarters, ed.), you can't get rid of the BOQ odor. They looked pretty good with paint and a little bit of paneling, and the air conditioning we put in there helped, but they still smelled like an old BOQ."[11]

Next, the MSC team assembled the fleet of aircraft and maintenance crews needed to support the astronaut flight training that would be done at Ellington. MSC Director Gilruth established an independent Aircraft Operations Office to coordinate the astronaut training with Air Force Reserve and Air National Guard based at Ellington, as well as the Air Force Systems Command headquarters. NASA arranged to transfer four F-102 fighter jets and two T-33 jet trainers from other bases to Ellington through the Air Force System Command. Kelly Air Force Base helped to get the program started by loaning a group of maintenance technicians to Ellington Air Force Base until NASA could get its own maintenance crew assembled. By September of 1962, all of the airplanes had arrived, the maintenance crews were in place, and the Manned Spacecraft Center began astronaut training at Ellington.[12]

By 1968, the MSC operated 42 active vehicles which flew a combined total of about 1,000 hours a month. By 1978, the MSC inventory included fighter jets, heavy equipment transport planes, helicopters and Lunar Landing vehicles. The Aircraft Operation Office at Ellington was responsible for routine maintenance for most of them. A crew of about 200 contract maintenance employees maintained the fleet and 23 aircraft inspectors from the Aircraft Quality Assurance Office monitored the fleet. Both offices operated out of Ellington.

Support systems and training modules connected with the Space program were scattered all over the United States, requiring the astronauts and crews to fly back and forth from these sites frequently. Their aircraft were housed in hangars at Ellington, and the crews took off and landed there. Take offs and landings had been the most precarious times during flight for pilots since the beginning of aviation. World War I era Ellington Field saw its share of crashes, and Ellington Air Force Base saw its share of crashes as well. Even pilots as highly trained as astronauts were subject to human error. On a clear Texas morning in February of 1966, four astronauts in training took off from Ellington to St. Louis to train on the rendezvous simulator in St. Louis, Missouri. Only two returned.[13]

Astronauts Elliot See (1927-1966) and Charles Bassett II (1931-1966) were backup pilots on Gemini IX mission for main pilots Thomas Stafford (1930-) and Eugene Cernan (1934-). One bright winter morning, the last day of February 1966, the Gemini IX foursome checked into Ellington Air Force Base, Texas, for flight clearance to St. Louis in two T-38 jet aircraft. They took off from Ellington at 7:35 A.M. See and Bassett led, with Stafford and Cernan flying wing position. Reaching St. Louis just before 9 o'clock in the morning, See learned that the visibility had dropped. As the aircraft descended through the uncertain weather, the pilots found themselves too far down the runway to land. See elected to keep the field in sight and he circled to the left underneath the cloud cover. Stafford climbed to make another instrument approach. He landed safely on his next attempt.

Meanwhile, See continued his left turn. The aircraft angled toward McDonnell Building 101, where technicians were working on the very spacecraft See and Bassett were scheduled to fly. See and Bassett's aircraft struck the roof of the building and crashed into a courtyard. Both pilots were killed.[14]

The Lunar Landing Training Vehicles were wingless, free-flying vehicles used to simulate the final 500 feet of a lunar landing. Astronauts practiced vertical takeoffs and landings in them before every lunar mission. First, though, they had to learn how to fly the new vehicles, and often practiced on the runways at Ellington. On May 7, 1968, Safety Engineer Richard H. Holzapfel sent the following priority memorandum to the NASA Administration after the LLRV#1 (Lunar Landing Research Vehicle) crashed at Ellington Air Force Base, Texas.

> Pilot Neil A. Armstrong NAS, MSC Astronaut, ejected after apparent loss of control. Armstrong incurred minor laceration to tongue. Vehicle was on standard lunar landing training mission. Estimated altitude at time of ejection 200 feet. LLRV#1 total loss—First estimate $1.5 million dollars....[15]

Sgt. Joe Briggs, who was stationed at Ellington, had a much more dramatic recollection of the accident. He was observing the flight from a F-102 airplane when he noticed the lunar vehicle flying at an odd angle. A mere few seconds later, the powerful ejection system in the lunar craft shot the pilot several hundred feet into the air, then exploded and crashed.[16]

The loss of the LLV was balanced by the safe landing of pilot and astronaut Armstrong.

The number of buildings the Manned Spacecraft Center occupied on base grew from 14 to 98 over the years, and the MSC became the single largest tenant at Ellington Air Force Base. The 2578th Air Base Squadron of the Continental Air Command (CONAC) at Ellington was the "host" or leasing agent for the contract between NASA and the Air Force. As host agent, the squadron provided manpower for security, fire protection, aircraft support, base operations, policing service, transient alert and transportation, maintenance for the building, grounds, and vehicles, crash and rescue support. The most significant support the Air Force squadron supplied was the flight crew operations, since all the MSC aircraft were located on and maintained at Ellington. For these services, NASA reimbursed the Air Force an estimated $309, 578 in 1968. [17]

Ellington Air Force Base was the site from which the research for many technological advances was launched. Besides the astronaut training and support for the programs at the MSC, NASA was involved in other scientific endeavors. NASA's fleet of five high-altitude airplanes supported the Earth Resources Division of the Goddard Space Flight Center in Maryland, and the research of a number of universities in developing the science of predicting crop production, monitoring salt infiltration of the soil and insect infestations, tracking deforestation and other investigations.[18] Later, NASA would be associated with Project Airstream, a long-term NASA/ Department of Energy multidisciplinary study of the upper atmosphere, and the high-flying WB-57 airplane stationed at Ellington would be used to collect "cosmic dust" for the Solar System Exploration Division at the MSC. [19] Experiments performed by NASA impacted the development of inventions as commonplace as television, The NASA newspaper, *Space News Roundup,* enthusiastically reported the latest innovation made possible by space exploration, Communications by laser beam from the fringes of space is the goal of a two-month long series of tests....being carried out through the use of a WB-57 aircraft operating at 60,000 feet....The plane, operated by MSC from Ellington AFB, flies over the ground station located on Redstone Arsenal, Alabama....Principal objective of the ...flight tests is to determine the effects of the atmosphere on vertical transmission of laser beams....Theoretically, up to a million television channels can be broadcast simultaneously over a single laser from space."[20]

Keep Them Flying

Pride in workmanship and service imbued NASA/JSC employees with a sense of mission even in the routine procedures, as indicated by the following article out of the JSC weekly newspaper entitled, "Keeping them Flying, "Sometime in the near future, NASA's T-38 fleet will surpass a combined total of 200,000 flying hours, equal to almost 23 years in the air, seven days a week, 24 hours a day....NASA got its first T-38 24 years ago, and the fleet is still going strong because of a crew of about 230 workers at Ellington Field ...." [21]

NASA T-38 Aircraft on Runway at Ellington Field, Courtesy of JSC Digital Image Collection

Dr. Story Musgrave, the man who has flown more hours in a T-38 than anyone on earth, commented on the contributions of the crews at Ellington: "The best maintenance in the world. Our engines are better kept and better tuned than anyone's." The superior design of the plane did not diminish the outstanding flying record held by NASA's fleet of T-38s, and the superb performance of the fleet came down to the dedication of the hands that have worked on them over the years. Maintenance standards for the T-38s at Ellington were far above standards required anywhere else. The preflight checklist at Ellington had more critical items on it than even the Air Force's checklist. For the Ellington mechanics, one engine problem was one problem too many. Many of the mechanics at Ellington had worked on

T-38s since the airplane first came into existence, and knew the airplane design, strengths and weaknesses inside and out. Many of the mechanics stayed with the program for years and years.[22]

On February 17, 1973, NASA renamed the Manned Spacecraft Center the Lyndon B. Johnson Space Center, which became commonly referred to as the JSC. Even a program with as much public appeal and excitement as the exploration of space was not immune to budgetary cuts. Therefore, the Johnson Space Center created opportunities to keep the public excited about its programs by inviting the public to ceremonies, air shows, and space flight-related displays held at Ellington Field. For example, in January of 1978, the Boeing 747 airplane used transport the Space Shuttle aircraft back and forth from Florida to California needed to make a refueling stop. Robert A. Newman, then Director of Public Affairs at the NASA office in Washington, D.C., considered how this move might be used to get the public excited about the space program. He proposed that the refueling be done at Ellington Air Force Base so the general public, the media, and NASA employees could view the shuttle-carrying airplane and the shuttle itself.[23]

Armed Forces Week in May offered another opportunity to show off all the aircraft based at Ellington and demonstrate their capabilities. Every year, the Base invited the public, free of charge, to watch precision flying demonstrations by the U.S. Navy's Blue Angels, a maximum performance takeoff by a Lockheed C-130 cargo plane or flyovers of F-101 and F-4 Phantom jets. Visitors could climb inside the cockpits of Coast Guard, Marine Corps, and Army helicopters parked on the runway. NASA allowed close-up inspection of the T-38 Talon training jets used by the astronauts, the Grumman Gulfstream shuttle training aircraft, a Boeing high-altitude WB-57, the modified KC-135 zero-gravity training airplane, and the B-377 "Super Guppy" cargo aircraft. NASA and the Texas Air National Guard had colorful displays open in Hangar 594.[24]

The Deactivation of Ellington Air Force Base

Ellington Air Force Base was the only active-duty Department of Defense installation in southeast Texas in 1970. By this time, the military operations on base shared runway space and flight time with NASA training. There were ninety aircraft stationed at the base, and that year they performed 200,000 flight operations. Forty-eight astronauts flew at Ellington, and all Lunar Landing Vehicle (LLV) trainings were conducted at Ellington. The base was the preferred landing area for military and civilian dignitaries for reasons of security, and all the NASA astronauts celebrated their return to earth at Ellington.[25] The Department of the Air Force had considered deactivating Ellington as an Air Force Base since 1966, but the needs of the expanding space program at nearby Johnson Manned Spacecraft Center and the uncertainties of the Cold War kept Ellington active. In 1974, the Air Force announced that Ellington would be closed by the summer of 1976, and all units would be transferred to Kelly Air Force Base in San Antonio and Bergstrom Air Force Base in Austin.

The protests against the base closing were vehement. Protestors included retired Maj. Gen. Vincent Chiodo, James White, the state commander of the American Legion, C.H. Taylor, with the Military Affairs Committee of the Houston Chamber of Commerce. In 1975, Gov. Dolph Briscoe invoked a little-used law and refused to allow the Air Force to relocate a National Guard unit, thus temporarily delaying the closing of Ellington Air Force Base. An article in *The Houston Post* newspaper declared, "The 147th Fighter –Interceptor Air National Guard Unit at Ellington is responsible for helping protect the petro-chemical industry along the Texas Gulf Coast and is the only unit between New Orleans and San Antonio."[26]

Air Force budget cutbacks forced closing of the base in March, 1976, when it became the property of the Air National Guard. The 147th Fighter Interceptor Group (ANG) was designated by the Air Force to phase-down Ellington AFB. The last student of combat training graduated 4 May 1976. For the next eight years, National Guard operated the base, and it was used primarily by the Guard and as a training facility for NASA. The once-mighty Ellington Air Force Base was demoted to plain Ellington Field, declared surplus property, and put for sale or lease by the General Services Administration of the Federal government.

Astronaut Training at Ellington Includes Women

In 1977, NASA announced that it was going to train a new class of astronauts, the first in eight years. The first group included six female astronaut candidates out of a class of thirty. John E. McLeaish, Chief of the

NASA Public Information Office from 1969-1977, recalled trying to publicize the idea that NASA was selecting women: "I was talking to Dan Rather trying to sell him on the idea of a *60 Minutes* thing with the women, which he found interesting, but I think they finally decided not to do it. But I figured that was worth a pitch."[27] Since then, forty-three women have become NASA astronauts, including Dr. Mae Jemison, the first African American woman in space.[28] All of these women polished their flying and aviation skills at Ellington Field.

One of the outstanding women in the Space program who did the astronaut training at Ellington was aerospace engineer and pilot Lt. Col. Stephanie Wells. She flew T-38s as an active duty officer in the Air Force from 1975-1985, and in the Air Force Reserves at Kelly Field, Texas, from 1985-1995. She accepted an assignment to work for NASA at the Johnson Space Center at Ellington Field in 1995. Her duties included being Aviation Safety Officer for the field and flight instructor for the astronauts and mission specialists. She trained astronauts in the T-38 training aircraft. All pilot-astronauts are routinely checked out in the T-38s, and fly it to maintain their flying skills. Mission specialists learned about aviation in general—avionics, navigation, communication, aircrew coordination—everything they needed to know to operate in a dynamic high-performance environment.

Lt. Col. Wells also flew the C-135 and the Gulfstream G-2, four of which were modified as shuttle and astronaut training aircraft (STA's). As Lt. Col. Wells explained, "The STAs are also for astronaut training. Highly modified business jets, they're designed to model the Shuttle during the descent and landing phase. Each pilot astronaut practices many hundreds of shuttle approaches, (called 'dives' since they are so steep) in the STA before they ever go into space. It's like an airborne simulator." The fifth Gulfstream G-2 she flew regularly was not modified. It was used for mission support, primarily flying NASA managers and officials to mission-related business around the country and around the world. She was one of the pilots who flew the Columbia Shuttle Disaster investigators to and from the salvage sites and meetings.[29]

The KC-135 Wells flew was used for astronaut training, both for Zero-Gravity training as well as heavy aircraft training. On a typical flight, it flew forty "parabolas," which created about twenty-five seconds of microgravity on each maneuver. The astronauts used the brief periods of zero gravity to test their working abilities in a low gravity environment, and also to test various pieces of hardware before they were used in space.[30] This was the aircraft that earned the nickname, the "Vomit Comet".

Ellington Field Hangs On

Although Ellington Field was no longer an active military base, there was still considerable value in the runways and hangars, and the strategic location of the airfield near the ports of Houston and Galveston. The growing petroleum industry kept the argument about the status of the airfield going in political circles. In a visit to Ellington in 1978, President Jimmy Carter announced the base was too important for the nation's security to be sold. President Carter said, " The decision to retain Ellington will allow this most important work to continue... We need more time to determine the best future of this valuable property."[31] Furthermore, the Space Program was big business in Texas, and the presence of NASA in Houston brought money, prestige, and considerable political leverage to the state. Ellington could not be completely abandoned because NASA needed the facility for its astronaut training program. By 1979, NASA had occupied its buildings at Ellington for almost eighteen years- far beyond the "temporary" use it originally planned. After long deliberations about the value of rehabilitating the World War II era buildings that housed its offices on Ellington, NASA declared a "continuing long-term need" for its facilities and dedicated $1,700,000 for repairs and rehabilitation of its facilities at Ellington Field.[32] On June 10, 1980 Texas Governor W.P. Clements designated July 14-20, as Space Week in Texas, and a grass-roots coalition of local businesses, flying clubs, and schools provided programs, lectures and displays under the theme "Space For Your Future" at Johnson Space Center.

In 1981, the Reagan Administration considered Ellington as a possible site for a refugee detention center. Government sources confirmed that Ellington was one of five military sites being considered to house illegal Haitians, Cubans and other refugees.[33] The Houston City Council passed a resolution of intent to acquire Ellington for aviation purposes, opposing the federal proposal to use the site for a refugee center.[34] Officials of the Air Force and General Services Administration then removed Ellington from the list of possible detention center sites.[35] The General Services Administration (GSA) released the major portion of Ellington for use as a public airport. The City of Houston and City of Pasadena became rivals for the valuable property.[36] When the Federal Government awarded most of the Ellington property to the City of Houston for use as a general aviation site, [37] the mayor of Pasadena tried to stop transfer.[38] In 1984, the property was purchased by the City of Houston Department of Aviation as an Auxiliary field, and the City of Houston received a $550,000 federal grant to improve and update the runways. The General Services Administration awarded 107 acres and golf course on Ellington property to City of Pasadena.

Houston Airport System

The City of Houston acquired 1,658 acres, the bulk of the Ellington Field land, for general aviation operations, runway, and railroad access on July 1, 1984. [39] The buildings on the City's portion of the property were old, run down, and had been empty since 1976. They were further damaged by hurricane Alicia in 1983. For two years after its purchase, the City of Houston invested nothing in the property they had lobbied so hard to get. Local newspapers began running articles about the dilapidated buildings and junk that was left to rot on the city's portion of the base. Finally, in 1986, demolition began on thirty-six buildings, including the barracks, officers club, bowling alley, two swimming pools, warehouses, a maintenance hangar and administration buildings.

Ellington Field became part of the Houston Airport System, and was developed as an auxiliary field to Hobby and Intercontinental airports. The goal was to use the runways at Ellington to relieve some of the traffic congestion at both major fields by handling the cargo, commuter and private charter flights. The new ownership meant major changes for the Field's other tenants. For the first time, there would be a daily mix of flights by light aircraft and high performance jets. Because of the wide variation in takeoff speeds, air traffic control at Ellington suddenly became much more complicated. The National Aeronautics and Space Administration (NASA), which operated the Johnson Space Center (JSC), and the other tenants at Ellington had to adapt quickly.

In 1984, NASA still had 31 airplanes based at Ellington Field, the largest inventory of aircraft of all the NASA centers. The U.S. Coast Guard had helicopters based at the field. The addition of general aviation, commercial and cargo flights for the Houston Airport System meant four or five times as many flights taking off and landing on the runways at Ellington Field every day, and safety became the major concern. NASA Johnson Space Center (JSC) Safety officer Roger Zweig offered this solution: "...we can help people understand the potential conflicts. For example, we can suggest that all slow airplanes use the same runway and the fast planes use a different one....The new flights will make it more like driving your car into Houston during rush hour."[40]

The changes at the airfield coincided with plans the Johnson Space Center was making to upgrade all its facilities at Ellington. When the JSC, then called the Manned Spacecraft Center (MSC), first located at Ellington AFB in 1962, they anticipated occupying the buildings for only one or two years, and were reluctant to invest much capital in rehabilitating the old buildings. By 1984, after twenty-two years of continuous occupation, JSC's initial investment had proven its wisdom, but the base was in serious need of a complete overhaul. The JSC rehabilitated the post-war buildings it occupied at Ellington Field, and the electrical and mechanical systems and concrete surfaces from 1984 to 1987.[41]

The first "Wings Over Houston" air show was held in the fall of 1984 by an organization then known as the Confederate Air Force, now called the Commemorative Air Force. The non-profit organization was dedicated to preserving America's aviation history through its preservation of World War II aircraft. The ten-day Flight Festival became an annual event at Ellington. In 1991, the air show drew 150,000 people to Ellington Field, and attracted so much interest from aviation enthusiasts that the show promoters began turning exhibitors down. The 1991 show included the first exhibit of the Stealth Fighter in Houston, the first-ever B-52 landing at Ellington, NASA training vehicles, and aircraft as diverse as an Iraqi-fired Scud missile to a talking clown helicopter.[42]

In 1987, commercial business at the airport began to pick up. Grumman leased 66 acres to build its Space Systems Operations Division, and United Parcel Service moved its air cargo operations to Ellington. In 1989, the U.S. Department of Transportation gave the City of Houston a $1 million grant for work on the runway approaches.[43] The investment paid off in 1990, when the first commercial flight for Continental Express took off from the runway at Ellington. In 1991, the Federal Aviation Improvement Administration granted $5 million to the City of Houston for capital improvements at Ellington. An economic report compiled in 1998 for the Houston Airport System reported that Ellington Field generated $233 million in earnings, dollars spent and re-spent in the local economy.[44]

End Notes

[1] Dave W. Lang, *The Impact of The Manned Spacecraft Center on the Houston Gulf Coast Area* (Houston: National Aeronautics and Space Administration, 1967), 2.

[2] Ibid., 5.

[3] Ibid., 4.

[4] "Housing and Community Housing Requirements of NASA Manned Spacecraft Center", editor Howard N. Martin, p. 10, states that by June of 1963 there were 2,760 persons employed at the MSC, and their families, for a total of 9,300 people. In these families, there were 4,500 children.

[5] Roy C. Aldridge, interview by Robert B. Merrifield. October 22, 1968. Oral History transcript, Merrifield Box 1. Johnson Space Center History Collection, University of Houston Clear Lake Archives, 2.

[6] Dave W. Lang, interview by Robert B. Merrifield., December 12, 1967. Oral History transcript, Merrifield Box 2, Johnson Space Center History Collection, University of Houston Clear Lake Archives, 7, 8.

[7] Ibid., 8, 9.

[8] Roy C. Aldridge, interview, 2.

[9] Lang interview, 8.

[10] Martin A. Byrnes, jr.,, interview by Robert B. Merrifield, Dec. 12, 1967. Oral History transcript, Merrifield Box 1, JSC History Collection, 15, 34.

[11] Lang interview, 13.

[12] Joseph S. Algranti, interview by Robert B. Merrifield, March 28, 1968, Oral History transcript, Merrifield Box 1, JSC History Collection, 2, 3.

[13] Barton C. Hacker and James M. Grimwood, *On the Shoulders of Titans: A History of the Gemini Project* (Washington, D.C. Scientific and Technical Office, National Aeronautics and Space Administration, 1977), 323, 324.

[14] Ibid.

[15] Richard H. Holzapfel to B.P. Helgerson, J.F. Lederer, May 7, 1968, Memorandum. JSC History Collection.

[16] CMSGT. Joe Briggs, interview by author, May 16, 2007.

[17] Dr. George E. Mueller, letter from Robert R. Gilruth, June 12, 1968, Renegotiation Packet, JSC History Collection.

[18] Dean Franklin Grimm, interview by Carol Butler, August 17, 2000. Oral History transcript, JSC History Collection, 95.

[19] *Space News Roundup*, January 1, 1984. Vol. 27, No. 1. JSC History Collection, 2.

[20] *Space News Roundup*, September 1, 1972. JSC History Collection, 4.

[21] *Space News Roundup*, August 26, 1988. Vol. 27, No. 24, JSC History Collection, 3.

[22] *Space News Roundup*, August 26, 1988. Vol. 27, No. 24, JSC History collection, 3.

[23] Memorandum from Robert A. Newman to Robert McCormick, January 4, 1978, Folder SHU 015-56. JSC History Collection.

[24] *Space News Roundup*, May 19, 1982. Vol. 21, No. 10, JSC History Collection.

[25] Fact Sheet, Ellington Air Force Base, Texas. Ellington Air Force Base, office of the Base Historian, 1970.

[26] *The Houston Post,* August 8, 1975.

[27] John E. McLeaish, interview by Rebecca Wright, November 15, 2001. Oral History Transcript, JSC History Collection. 72.

[28] For a complete list of women astronauts, see Appendix 4.

[29] Stephanie Wells, interview by author at Pe-Te's Restaurant Across from Ellington Field April 8, 2002.

[30] *Woman Pilot Magazine,* "Swinging on A Star", http://www.womanpilot.com.

[31] *The Houston Post,* June 24, 1978.

[32] Billie J. McGarvey, Director of Facilities, NASA, Washington, D.C., to Earl E. Jones, Assistant Commissioner, Office of Real Property, General Services Administration, Washington, D.C., September 12, 1979. JSC History Collection.

[33] *The Houston Post,* June 13,1981.

[34] *Houston Chronicle,* June 19, 1981.

[35] *The Houston Post,* July 8, 1981.

[36] *The Houston Post,* October 8, 1981

[37] *Houston Chronicle,* June 16, 1982.

[38] *Houston Chronicle,* August 24, 1982.

[39] "Ellington Field Master Plan Study Prepared For the City of Houston, Texas," (Bedford, New Hampshire: Hoyle, Tanner & Associates, Inc., 1987), Sec. 2, 4.

[40] *Space News Roundup*, August 3, 1984. Vol. 23, No. 14. JSC History Collection, 3.

[41] Ibid.

[42] *Space News Roundup,* October 25, 1991. Vol. 30, No. 42. JSC History Collection, 4.

[43] *The Houston Post,* September 9, 1989.

[44] *1998 Economic Impact Study,* Houston Airport System, .3.

CHAPTER VII

Ellington in the 21st Century

In 2001, Ellington Field began to function as a base of operations for the newly created National Department of Homeland Security Program under the administration of the Texas Air National Guard. The proximity of the Port of Houston, the Johnson Space Center, the massive Texas Medical Center complex, and the petrochemical industry to the fourth most populous city in the United States[1] meant that Houston was just as likely a target for Middle Eastern terrorism in the 21st Century as it was for German U-Boats during World War II or Russian ballistic missiles during the Cold War that began in the 1950's. The similarity of the perception of imminent danger to Houston and the Gulf Coast as expressed in 1951 by Col. K.K. Black, then commander of the 158th ACWG at Ellington Air Force Base, and in 2001 by Col. Steve Jones, Vice Wing Commander of the 147th Fighter Interceptor Group at Ellington, clearly demonstrated the continual need for strategic defense of the area. In his interview in 1951, Col. Black commented, "As a strategic industrial center, Houston would be the Number 1 target of enemy bombers in a war with Russia.... Texas is the Number 1 state in point of strategic materials, both raw and processed.... And therefore in event of war, the industrial concentrations of this region and state might be in as great danger from...sabotage.... Military defense, civil defense and coordination of the two are imperative. But precautionary defenses against sneak attacks from within are of potentially equal urgency."[2]

In 2001, less than a month after the terrorist attack on the World Trade Center in New York, Col. Jones explained the ongoing mission of the147th Fighter Interceptor Group, "...our mission has remained the same, and that's the air sovereignty, air superiority, air defense of the south, southeast region of the United Sates, and the Gulf coast and the Houston petrochemical base.... Anything that falls into that area...we treat it the same way, and we would prosecute and intercept on anything that seemed to be a threat to anything in that region."[3] The names of the countries at war with the United States might have changed over the years, but the threat of attack and the need for a prompt and decisive military response had not changed.

Col. Jones' words regarding the duty of the Fighter Interceptor Group at Ellington Field to defend the nation's resources were put into immediate action on September 11, 2001. After the terrorist attack, the 147th Fighter Group (FIG) stationed at Ellington Field called up an additional 125 personnel to active duty in the unit to provide a 24-hour-a-day, 7-day-a-week safety net for Houston and the Gulf Coast area, and two of the unit's F-16 fighter jets were positioned on the runway at Ellington Field, with their fuel tanks topped off and armaments on the ready. The crew can be on the planes and in the air within minutes of any emergency, 24 hours a day.

Impact of Being Called to Active Duty on Texas Families

In the military, national emergencies and disasters cause a ripple effect of call ups to active duty until the manpower (and womanpower) is sufficient to deal with the crisis over time. The hardship that soldiers and their families endure when they are unexpectedly called up into military service for undetermined periods of time has existed since the Revolutionary War in the earliest days of our country, and the sacrifice has remained from war to war until the most recent times. In October of 2001, four hundred Texas National Guardsmen were called up to secure twenty-six commercial airports in Texas, and an additional five hundred soldiers assigned to the 49th Armored Division were called up for processing and training. Many of these men, and increasingly women, had spouses and children who were suddenly faced with the absence of one or more parents for a long time. Each one of these men and women held a regular civilian job that had to be covered by co-workers. Massive military call-ups like this one in Texas took place in every state and put a burden on families and businesses across the entire country. Employee loss was especially hard on small businesses. Lt. Col. Bob Luna, Public Affairs Officer of the Texas National Guard stationed at Camp Mabry in Austin, Texas, recognized the burden on the soldiers, their families, and employers:

> We want to thank the employers for supporting this call, because… all of a sudden this individual is gone, for what could be a week to two years….The families take a toll also, because all of a sudden the individual that would come home every day for supper…is not coming home for supper for a while. Once they are activated, they are paid active duty pay. Each individual gets paid by his or her rank, and the number of years that they have in the military, so everybody is different. And granted, you might have a president of a bank that might make $8,000 a month but in the National Guard he might be a Lieutenant, and he'll be making maybe $2,000 a month."[4]

Sacrifice has ever been the price of freedom, which was no surprise to any of the generations of citizen soldiers of the National Guard or Reserves who answered repeated calls to the service of their country throughout the years. The sacrifices mentioned by Col. Luna in 2001 were reflected many years earlier in a 1958 letter from Col. K.K. Black to his congressman which revealed the personal cost of his service as a reservist, at a time when there were no employer/employee relief laws to protect the soldiers or businesses from financial ruin. Col. Black wrote:

> After serving five and one half years in World War II, I returned to civilian life to re-establish my (navigation) instrument business; having declined a regular appointment, but retaining my reserve status in the Air Force as Lt. Colonel. After several years of hard work and financial sacrifices I finally returned my business to a paying and growing basis. Almost immediately thereafter I was involuntarily recalled to active duty for service in Korea and elsewhere.
>
> Under the law enacted by Congress I was obligated to remain on active duty for only two years, which would have released me in August 1953. However, six months prior to that date I was required to indicate my willingness to remain on active duty for an indefinite period of time. At this time, the Korean fracas was still in full swing and it did not appear logical for me to go back

> to my business (or another one) with the distinct possibility hanging over my head of almost immediate recall to fight a full scale war with Russia. In the meantime, without my personal supervision and guidance, my business had deteriorated almost to the point of insolvency. I later sold out completely and my real losses, resulting from my involuntary recall to active duty, exceeded $45,000.00...
>
> Insofar as patriotic motivation is concerned my record will indicate service, with modest distinction, in all of my assignments...I have faithfully maintained military readiness for over thirty years. [5]

Col. Black's grandson faced the same disruption in a different war. MSGT Troy Meredith was called to active duty as a reservist from October of 2001 to December of 2002, again in April of 2003, and several times thereafter. He wrote to his aunt about his service: [6]

> I got back from the last mission [to Afghanistan] on Thursday [May 23] and I have to leave again tomorrow so there's not much time to do anything. I was activated on Oct. 15, 2001 for one year. It is considered a temporary activation, which means by the current regulations they can extend that for another year.... Word is that the war is on and they may change the rules and keep us on active duty for as long as they need us. Not good news but, I stayed in the reserves for patriotic reasons.... I am in federal civil service so my job will be there when I get off active duty. While on active duty.... I do lose my contributions to my retirement fund.... Initially I took a pretty good size pay cut. Since I live 150 miles away from the base.... I closed down my apartment down.... Also, I fly out of country frequently.... My goal before activation was to be hired as a Border Patrol pilot....Because I am gone so much I haven't been able to finish. This hurts me the most because my goal came to screeching halt. The chief pilots in the sectors I will apply to know that I am on active duty, so even if I am qualified they won't hire me.... I could probably press the military issue but .... I have chosen not to take that route. It is just going to have to wait until this is over....

The examples of Col. Black and his grandson were only two of thousands of stories of military service, just as the history of Ellington Field is the history of only one of hundreds of military bases that have come, served their purpose and gone. The thousands of men and women who were trained at Ellington Field over the last eighty-five years were part of the vast national legacy of service to our country. After an act of international terrorism had left its ugly scar in New York in 2001, Ellington Field's future as a necessary and strategic part of the air defense of the Gulf Coast region and the nation seemed assured. However, as with all things military, change was once again on the horizon.

The New Century

In the year 2000, Mary Case, who was at the time the Ellington Airport Manager for the Houston Airport System (HAS), stated that all of the current tenants at Ellington had indicated that they would remain for the foreseeable future,[7] and Duane Ross, Director of Astronaut Training at the Johnson Space Center, reported that NASA would continue to use Ellington Field to house and maintain the fleet of airplanes used by the astronauts, and as a landing and flight training field.[8]

The Texas Air National Guard and the Texas Army National Guard were also on duty at Ellington, occupying the northern section of the field. The 147th fighter jet that was installed in 1995 still rose symbolically into the sky on its pole. The young Lieutenant who had flown it while he was a member of the Texas Air National Guard's 147th FIG from May 27, 1968 to October 1, 1973, was George W. Bush,[9] now President of the United States. President Bush was the first member from the 147th Group to attain the country's highest office.

George Bush plane from Authors Collection

On September 11, 2001, a flight of Ellington's F-16's played a crucial role in the nation's defense. The 147th Fighter Wing scrambled its aircraft to help ensure control of our country's airspace during those first chaotic hours after the attack on the Twin Towers. The Wing's 111th Fighter Squadron, the President's own unit from his Texas Air National Guard days, formed a protective escort for President Bush and Air Force One as they flew the President out of harm's way on a top-secret route across the country that day. The squadron also escorted the President's plane back to Washington, D.C. The 147th continued to perform air cover operations in post-9/11 New York.

Public events on Ellington remained very popular and continued to be scheduled unless the current political situation prevented free access. The base continued participate in the Johnson Space Center annual open house in August, which was attended by more than 100,000 people in the year 2000. However, the terrorist attack on the World Trade Center in New York City in 2001 forced the cancellation of the JSC Open House for 2002, and temporarily restricted other public events and access to the JSC.

According to the HAS Ellington Field Master Plan Update prepared in 2002,[10] the airfield could accommodate a substantial increase in aviation activity and development. The plan suggested that an additional 50 acres of land be reserved for future expansion, and identified 650 acres of vacant land available for future development at Ellington Field. Dr. Kent McLemore, Assistant Director of Aviation for the Houston Airport System, and also the Planning Director, reviewed the Master Plan and mapped the various sites the HAS was considering for future light industrial, heavy industrial, and commercial office space. Part of Dr. McLemore's job was to explore ways to attract new businesses and industries to Ellington Field.[11]

One of the most exciting potential future uses for a parcel of the vacant land at Ellington Field was the possibility that a National Veterans Museum would be developed and built there. The project was begun in 2001 by a group of Houston citizens, headed by Houston resident and Vietnam veteran Malcolm Browne. By December of 2002, the museum committee had plans for a three-story building with 203,000 square feet of exhibit, library, theater and office space. The building design featured five wings in a star shape, with each wing dedicated to one particular branch of the service. Houston City Councilman Michael Berry summarized the argument for the museum to be at Ellington:

> It makes no sense to leave land vacant at Ellington Field rather than encourage a $100 million investment of private money to attract local and out-of-state tourism, provide an educational opportunity, and honor the valor of our nation's veterans.... This is the right project, at the right time, and Ellington Field is the right place for it—and I'm calling on veterans and supporters of this project to help make this happen...here we're only asking to give our veterans—the men and women who answered the call to duty to defend our freedom—the opportunity to raise private funds and build a public treasure. It's just the right thing to do.[12]

Despite tremendous local support and the obvious historic compatibility of building a museum for military veterans on vacant land at Ellington Field, negotiations with the Houston Airport System and the City of Houston for a museum site on Ellington were unproductive. The discussions became moot in 2004, when the museum project received an unexpected donation of a thirty-five acre tract of land from Exxonmobil Corporation about two miles north and west of Ellington. This tract put the museum location at the intersection of two major highways on highly visible, easily accessible commercial property.

In 2003, Ellington Field continued to serve as a joint-use civilian/military airport. It operated as a base for corporate, commercial, cargo and private aviation operations. There were three active runways and an air traffic control tower that operated 24 hours a day. Continental Express airline shared the site with The Texas Air National Guard, Texas Army National Guard, Coast Guard and NASA, who owned and operated sections of the base and paid an annual fee to the Houston Airport System for the use of the runways and amenities. Three smaller tenants, Cliff Hyde Flying Services, The Commemorative Air Force, and Southwest Airport Services also leased space at Ellington. United Parcel Service had a small fleet of Boeing 767 aircraft that flew cargo out of Ellington. Other tenants who occupied office space and land at Ellington included the Coast Guard, a flying service, and various aviation related companies and several smaller commercial businesses.

The Coast Guard also utilized runway space at the field. In an interesting coincidence in history, the Coast Guard was created the same time as Ellington Field. It was originally established in 1918 to combat the pirates who were terrorizing merchant ships along the coast in the Gulf of Mexico. The Coast Guard has continued to be an important asset to the busy maritime navigation and shipping industry, and one detachment still guards the Texas and Louisiana coastline from its station at Ellington Field. Coast Guard Air Station Houston at Ellington Field provides flight support for numerous search and rescue missions every year, along with other stations in Galveston, Freeport, Sabine Pass, and Houston. [13] The HH-52 helicopters, pilots, and enlisted men from the Air Station continued to serve the citizens of Houston and the entire gulf coast by responding to emergencies at sea. The unit performed many types of rescues from Ellington Field. For example, in 1999, the Coast Guard unit responded to 301 Search and Rescue emergencies. [14] In 2001, Air Station Houston rescued more than 80 people during and after Tropical Storm Allison. In 2003, unit helicopters flew Coast Guard environmental protection officers to the scene of an offshore oil well blowout in Trinity Bay. In July of 2004, a rescue team sent from the Air Station hoisted a diver from a dive boat 72 miles out to sea, and transported her to an ambulance waiting at Ellington Field. In March, 2005, another Air Station team rescued two fishermen from their rapidly sinking boat 30 miles southeast of Cameron, Louisiana.

Cliff Hyde Flying Services, which had been training pilots since before World War II, moved to Ellington in 1999. The company provided a two to three year flight instruction course designed to prepare pilots to fly commercial multi-engine airplanes. The Commemorative Air Force Gulf Coast Wing, which produces the annual "Wings Over Houston" air show every October at Ellington Field, continued to maintain a year-around office and hangar space. The objective of this nonprofit organization was to restore and maintain as complete a collection of vintage World War II combat aircraft as possible. Southwest Airport Services operated a full-service station for private aircraft and a refueling base for transient military aircraft. The number of other smaller aviation tenants leased all of the spaces with runway ramp frontage. Corporate tenants like Astrotechnology, Inc., BOMASADA Flight Operations, Sky Com, and North American Corporation occupied office space.

Despite a steady increase in the number of smaller tenants, the occupancy at Ellington dropped dramatically when Continental Express discontinued its flights from Ellington and United Parcel Service moved its cargo fleet to Bush Intercontinental Airport. To make matters worse, the Department of Defense Base Realignment and Closure Act (BRAC) and the National Guard Bureau were considering moving the Texas Air National Guard 147th FIG unit to another base in Texas. Finding new tenants to replace the ones who were leaving was a costly, slow process, and finding non-aviation related uses for airport property was very limited.

BRAC—The Base Realignment and Closure Act

In 1988, the Department of Defense (DOD) created the Base Realignment and Closure Commission (BRAC) to consolidate (realign) and streamline the nation's military installations and units to maximize military strength, eliminate redundant training and operations and make all the branches of the military more cost effective. The overall goal was to reduce the size of the military infrastructure and update the technology and equipment so the United States Armed Forces could remain a bulwark against the heightened threats the nation faced in the 21st century. The first round of base closings came during the Reagan administration, the second in the first Bush administration, and the third and fourth during President Clinton's term in office. These four rounds—in 1988, 1991, 1993, and 1997—resulted in ninety- seven major base closings and 290 other realignments to manpower and equipment placements. According to estimates from the Department of Defense, this restructuring saved the American taxpayers about $18 billion through fiscal year 2001 and a further $7 billion per year since.[15]

In 1997, former Defense Secretary William S. Cohen and military leaders in the DOD stressed that the United States Armed Forces must become more agile and flexible to face new challenges, and that there must be a consistent, continued effort to reposition U.S. military forces wherever they are most needed and most effective around the world. This commitment was reinforced in 2001 by Defense Secretary Donald H. Rumsfeld when he took office. Between December of 2003 and May of 2005, the DOD completed an exhaustive military force structure analysis, assessed the probable threats for the next twenty years, and compiled a world-wide inventory of the United State's military installations, manpower and equipment.[16] Based on this information, the BRAC then defined critical points of strategic importance and used these points as criteria to measure the value of each base worldwide. These criteria were then used to build a list of the military installations to be recommended for realignment[17] or closure. Every military installation was measured against the same criteria, and all were considered candidates for closure or realignment.

For communities whose existence began with or continued because of the building of a military base nearby, the impact of a base closure filtered into every segment of the local economy. A base closure meant hundreds or thousands fewer people in stores, gas stations, schools and churches and many homes for sale or rent. The larger the base, the more economic impact it had on the communities surrounding it. Communities surrounding these military bases often faced a major economic change, and in some cases, collapse when the bases were declared nonessential and closed.

Ellington Field was one of nineteen active military installations in the State of Texas in 2003, when the deadline for the BRAC process was announced. Right from the beginning, though, Ellington Field supporters faced a different challenge than most other military communities. Since Ellington Field was not an active-duty base, and was largely owned by the City of Houston, the only part of its operations that were threatened by the BRAC decision was the removal of the 147th Fighter Interceptor Group (FIG) and supporting National Guard personnel. All the other tenants, like the Houston Airport System and NASA, the two major users, would continue to operate there. The issue for Ellington was not one based primarily on economic impact either, since the other tenants would continue, or a worry about a complete closure, since it was a multi-use commercial airfield, and not solely a military airfield. The argument against the removal of the 147th, which may have seemed like an inconsequential item compared to some of the major base closings that were called for in the BRAC recommendations, was nevertheless one of the most important arguments to be presented before the BRAC committees. Ellington's small military presence was crucial, not to the local economy, but to the economy and security of the entire country. The presence of the 147th FIG at Ellington Field, Texas, was a matter of extreme and urgent importance to farmers in Iowa, Senators in Virginia, and households everywhere. The key task for the supporters of Ellington Field was making the politicians and military leaders in charge of the decision see that keeping the 147th FIG at Ellington

Field was not just a local issue, but an issue of national security and importance. Politicians might not be impressed that Houston was the fourth most populous city in the country, but they needed to consider that the petrochemical complex in the Greater Houston area produced nearly half of the nation's base petrochemicals[18]—which are used in the manufacturing of items used in every household, every day. The oil refineries along the Texas Gulf Coast also produced 3.83 million barrels of refined petroleum products every day—nearly one third of the U.S. total.[19] Houston is the leading domestic and international center for virtually every segment of the oil and gas industry, and for many of the nation's largest international engineering and construction firms.[20]

The 147th FIG maintained operational readiness not just for the defense of the immediate Houston area, but for the defense of the Gulf Coast region. If the proposed reduction went through, the Houston area would be left with only two to four jets at Ellington to scramble for intercept missions, with crews rotating in from other bases. Cost savings were not an issue, since savings from the proposed draw-down at Ellington were quite small. According to the BRAC Report,[21] the net present value of the costs and savings to the Department of Defense over the next 20 years is $3.6 million, or only $180,000 per year. Conversely, the losses were large-up to 556 full and part-time jobs could be forever lost in Houston if the 147th was realigned and sent elsewhere.[22]

BRAC'S Case

The condition of the fleet of F-16 aircraft the Air National Guard used at Ellington was on the verge of obsolescence. There were not enough surplus newer aircraft at other bases to swap into Ellington, and the cost of upgrading the equipment and extending the service life of the current fleet of 35 F-16's was a staggering $30,961,000 in 2004 and 2005 dollars.[23] The F-16 Falcon Fighter jets were slated for decommissioning, and without newer aircraft to replace them, the unit would not be able to continue in its prsent mission. Another factor was the availability of a fighter wing at San Antonio, which could be in the air over Houston in forty-five minutes. Unfortunately, for Houston in the case of a threat, forty five minutes might be tragically too late.

A Fight to Save the 147TH FIG at Ellington Begins

The Ellington Field Task Force is Formed

In 2003, the communities and businesses[24] surrounding Ellington Field joined forces and worked together through the Bay Area Houston Economic Partnership (BAHEP), to establish an Ellington Field Task Force (EFTF) with a mission to "Retain and grow military assets at Ellington Field with reference to the Base Realignment and Closure Process for 2005 (BRAC 2005)." It was the Task Force's intention to develop a plan to engage the citizens in the communities and key elected officials in an effective and active campaign to inform themselves about the BRAC process and the importance of keeping the 147th Fighter Wing at Ellington. Across the entire nation, most of the communities with military bases that would be impacted by the BRAC process had already developed very active BRAC 2005 committees to research the impact of closure and strategize effective counter proposals. Other communities in Texas recruited elected officials, community groups, business and industry leaders to actively lobby federal officials and military/homeland security committees in Washington, DC., as well as the Texas State officials and committee members in Austin. At least four of these other Texas communities included a proposal that the 147th Fighter Wing from Ellington be relocated to their own bases in their mission statements.

On February 25, 2003, the Ellington Field Task Force published a comprehensive proposal for the continuance of a military presence at Ellington Field. The Task Force promoted the development of Ellington Field as a Joint Reserve Base, in keeping with the "Future Forces" initiative that encouraged all branches of the Armed forces to work together, train together and where possible, eliminate the job redundancy created by having separate branches of the services. Over the next two years, there was a tremendous effort to alert the public and politicians to the potential loss of the 147th. Citizens, business owners and public officials from the surrounding communities became involved in the ongoing discussions, under the umbrella of the Bay Area Houston Economic Partnership, Task Force leaders spoke at the Texas Military Preparedness Commission, the Houston Military Affairs Committee, and local military organizations. The following entities passed resolutions of support for the Task Force: Harris County Commissioners Court, Port of Houston Authority, Greater Houston Partnership, Bay Area Houston Economic Partnership, Clear Lake Area Chamber of Commerce, Houston-Galveston Area Council, Galveston County Commissioners Court, and the communities of Taylor Lake, Pasadena, La Porte, Friendswood, Webster, and Santa Fe. [25]

The Port of Houston Authority's support was an acknowledgement of the 147th Fighter Wing's important role in protecting the port and the multi-billion dollar flow of goods in and out. The threat of a terrorist attack on the Port of Houston was very real, and one of the top concerns to national security. The Port Of Houston was the 6th busiest port in the world in 2005, and one of the two busiest ports in the United States. In 2005, 6,539 ships used the Port of Houston, and the Port handled 200 million short tons of goods. The value of those imported and exported goods was staggering. The leading trading partners were Mexico, with a dollar value of combined import and export goods of $7,767,510,25; Germany at $3,845,189,997; Venezuela at $3,245,788,097; Brazil at $3,110,147,978; and Saudi Arabia at $2,425,244,852.[26] An attack on the Port of Houston would directly and immediately impact the economies of at least thirty-one other countries.[27]

The Houston Airport System, the owner of most of Ellington Field and operator the entire airfield since 1984, also had a lot at stake in the event of the removal of the Air National Guard Wing. The steady, long term flow of fees from the Wing, and the services they provided for the entire base, such as fire protection, would not easily be replaced. Furthermore, the Wing occupied almost the entire north end of the field, so reusing the space would be a huge task. In a letter to Col. McNeely, Dr. Kent McLemore , Assistant Director of Aviation and Planning Manager, Houston Airport system (HAS), stated:

> It appears that any decrease in payments by the Air National Guard (ANG) will have to be made up by the Army, Coast Guard, NASA, and the Houston Airport System (HAS)... Any change in flight ops changes the amount paid by the remaining entities... If the ANG individual amount goes down due to decreased flight ops, then the formula would have to be refigured... and the cost redistributed among the Army, Coast Guard, NASA, and HAS. Ellington Field is already projected to have a $1.6

> million deficit for O&M in FY 2006... The net effect of a reduction in the ANGB amount will be an increased cost for HAS, which translates into an increase in the operating deficit of Ellington.[28]

The prospects for containing the cost of operating Ellington Field looked bleak, and the possibilities for finding a business with similar air industry related needs to replace the Fighter Wing looked even more remote.

The Future of Ellington Field

Ellington Field has been reborn time and time again and has continued to endure because the reasons why it is needed have not changed. War continues to be waged, industry, commerce and shipping continue to build along the coast, and the population of the gulf coast continues to increase. The NASA/Johnson Space Center has continued to operate out of Ellington Field for more than forty-five years. Air Force One, the plane used by United States presidents from Dwight D. Eisenhower (1890-1969) to George W. Bush (1946-SL) still lands safely on the runway at Ellington Field. Dignitaries visiting from all over the world land at Ellington when they come to Houston. Astronauts return to Ellington Field after orbiting the earth and moon. Space crews are still welcomed home in grand ceremonies at Ellington Field, as are the servicemen and women returning from tours of duty overseas.[29]

Since the Houston Airport System took over the majority of Ellington Field in 1984, it has been a "joint uses" airfield with military, City of Houston, and private tenants. By 2009, it will become a true "Joint Reserve" base, as well. This 54 million dollar expansion was the culmination of many months of work by the Ellington Field Task Force and Senator Kay Bailey Hutchison, Chairman of the Military Construction Appropriations Subcommittee, who initiated the process of moving the 2,500 troops from the Army's 75th Battle Command Training Division and the Navy and Marine Corps Reserve units from their location at the Old Spanish Trail Reserve Center in Houston to Ellington Field. The plans included building a $15 million dollar Armed Forces Reserve Center, a 6 million dollar Battle Projection facility for the Predator Drones that will be arriving at the base in 2007, and a new taxiway to be poured. Mr. Bob Mitchell,

Executive Director for the Bay Area Houston Economic Partnership, was quoted in an article in the *Citizen* newspaper: "Thanks to the work of Sen. Kay Bailey Hutchison, Ellington Field is evolving into a key economic development opportunity… The Ellington Field Task Force has been the driving force behind (the base's) survivability and growth."[30] In April of 2004, Senator Hutchison announced:[31]

"This is a great day for Ellington Field and the medical complex of Houston…. The plan will allow Army, Navy, and Marine Corps Reserves to better serve enlisted men and women and the taxpayers by enhancing Ellington's mission capabilities for our national defense…This expansion will bring jobs and economic activity to Houston and further enhance the research potential of the entire medical complex," The Senator added, "When Mayor White asked me to expedite this project, we put the pedal to the metal. I appreciate the Mayor's leadership in making it a priority for Houston."

Senator Hutchison was approached two years before by officials at M.D. Anderson Cancer Center[32], to determine if the Department of Defense would be amenable to moving the Reserve Center and allowing the land to be annexed for an expansion of the University of Texas Research Park. The world-class medical facility was growing rapidly and needed additional space.

Throughout the controversy about closure and realignment, the work of the 147th Fighter Wing and the Air National Guard at Ellington never ceased. The men and women from the unit continued to serve, and to be deployed. On February 23, 2007, the entire 147th Fighter Wing at Ellington was deployed to Iraq as part of Air Expeditionary Force 5/6. The unit's F-16 aircraft joined F-15, A-10, and B-1/52 aircraft from other bases and as many as 10,000 to 20,000 other personnel to support the war in Iraq.[33]

Joint Reserve Building going up, from Author's Collection

In June of 2007, the flat abandoned parade fields along the streets named for long- dead airmen again witnessed the Phoenix-like rise of mighty Ellington Field from the ashes of its past. Massive steel girders framed the sky for two large buildings, and bulldozers were shoving dirt aside for a new taxiway. Concrete trucks were coming and going, laying a more permanent future in their wake. In summary, for ninety years, Ellington Field has been an asset to Houston, the State of Texas, and to the Gulf coast, and the ever-vigilant guardian of our homes, our jobs, and our way of life. The men and women who served there will never be forgotten as long as there is one child who asks the question, "What did grandpa do in the war? " Recording part of the history of Ellington Field has been an honor and a privilege. May Ellington Field continue to endure and to serve and protect us all.

Joint Reserve Building going up, from Author's Collection

End Notes

[1] *Houston Facts 2005,* (Houston: Greater Houston Partnership Research Department, 2005), 3.

[2] Col. K.K. Black, interview in *Houston Chronicle* February 5, 1951.

[3] Colonel Steve Jones, interview by Paul Pendergraft, with KUHF 88.7 F.M. News, Tape recording, Oct. 9, 2001, transcription by author, December 1, 2001, in possession of the author.

[4] Lt. Col. Bob Luna, interview by Paul Pendergraft, KUHF 88.7F.M.News, Tape recording October 9, 2001, transcription by author, December 1, 2001, in possession of author.

[5] Letter regarding House Bill H.R 6994, dated April 17, 1957, proposing retention on active duty of those Reserve Officers who would have been mandatorily retired before achieving twenty years of service under Section 524 of the Reserve Officer's Personnel Act of 1954. Copy in possession of author.

[6] Msgt. Troy Meredith, 68th Airlift Squadron, 433rd Airlift Wing, U.S. Air Force Reserves, to Kathryn Black Morrow, Letter, dated May 27, 2002. .

[7] Mary Case, telephone interview by author, April 7, 2003.

[8] Duane Ross, telephone interview by author, March 10, 2003.

[9] See Biography section

[10] *Ellington Field Master Plan Update, Site Suitability Analysis* (San Francisco: Leigh Fisher Associates, 2002), 1.

[11] Dr. Kent McLemore, interview by author, March 12, 2003.

[12] Michael Berry, "Right Time, place for Vets Museum at Ellington," *Houston Chronicle Outlook*, December 26, 2002.

[13] U.S. Coast Guard, Group Galveston Homepage, at www.globalsecurity.org/military/agency/dot/gru_galveston.htm.

[14] Ibid.

[15] *BRAC 2005: Base Closure, Realignment Recommendations Follow Lengthy Process.* United States Department of Defense, American Forces Information Services, website www.defenselink.miol/news.

[16] *BRAC 2005: Base Closure, Realignment Recommendations Follow Lengthy Process.* "Defense Base Closure and Realignment Timeline. " United States Department of Defense, American Forces Information Services, website www.defenselink.miol/news. Accessed May 31, 2005.

[17] Realignment was a process of consolidating like missions and military training activities and redirecting the resources to current and future military needs.

[18] *Houston / Facts 2005,* 11.

[19] "Why Should The TX ANG 147th Fighter Wing Stay in Houston?" Bay Area Economic Partnership, Ellington Field Task Force website at www.supportellingtonfield.com.

[20] *Houston Facts 2005,* 10, 11.

[21] *BRAC 2005.*

[22] *Lonestar Times*, LonestarTimes.com, May 17. 2005, 1.

[23] Ibid., Section 1-1 Cost Data to Support 31 M to Support Service Life of Aircraft.

[24] Article, BRAC COMMISSION AND ELLINGTON FIELD, Houston Military Affairs Website, http://www.meplodet.com

[25] 147th Fighter Wing Electronic Book, Section 11-2.

[26] "Port of Houston Facts" Port of Houston Authority Website, http://www.portofhouston.com/busdev/tradestatistics.html, accessed June 2006. During the same period, the United States' top five exported commodities were Organic Chemicals at $7,537,902,037; Machinery at $5,479,202,458; Petroleum and Petroleum Products at $3,247,646,945; Plastics at $2,372,456,362; and Electric Machinery at $1,219,297,258.

[27] *Houston Facts 2005,* 10.

[28] Ibid., Section 20-1, emailed letter from Dr. Kent R. McLemore, Ph.D., AICP, dated 5 July, 2005.

[29] Johnson Space Center Announcement, March 16, 1989, Folder 89-050. JSC History Collection.

[30] *The Citizen,* December 28, 2006, 1, 11A.

[31] Press Release Office of Senator Kay Bailey Hutchison, dated April 1, 2004.

[32] M.D. Anderson Cancer Center is part of the world- famous Texas Medical Center in downtown Houston, which includes six general hospitals, eight specialized hospitals, four schools of nursing, two schools of pharmacy, a dental school and several degree-granting and post-doctoral plans of study. In 2004, the Texas Medical Center employed more than 62,000 people, including 4,000 doctors and 11,000 registered nurses, and covered 26 million square feet. *Houston Facts 2005,* 11. The presence of the Medical Center was another component of the argument for keeping the 147th FIG at Ellington.

[33] Ibid., March 1, 2007, 15A.

Biographies

The purpose of the biography section is to offer information on a few representative individuals who were mentioned on this book. All of them were at Ellington Field.

Lt. Eric Lamar Ellington (1889-1913)

Eric Ellington photo courtesy of Sam Drege Aerospace Museum, San Diego, CA

Eric Lamar Ellington, the son of Jessie and Sallie Williams Ellington, was born in Clayton, North Carolina, May 19, 1889. As a young boy, Eric developed a keen interest in military and naval history. When the Spanish-American War broke out, young Eric followed the progress of the campaigns with a degree of fervor and understanding that amazed his family. He and his brothers designed scale model ships and fought imaginary naval battles on the bedroom floor.[1]

At the age of sixteen, he was appointed to the United States Naval Academy in Annapolis, Maryland, where he excelled in his classes. He graduated seventh in a class of 230 students on June 5, 1909. In July of the same year he was assigned as a midshipman to the U.S.S. California, an armored cruiser. Young Ellington learned the skills necessary for a junior naval officer while aboard the cruiser; deck watch, navigation, signal operations, and administrative duties. Over the next two years, he developed his confidence and leadership skills, and in his final fitness report, was recommended for promotion to ensign.

In 1911, Ellington decided to transfer to the United States Army. After his transfer, he was assigned to the 3rd Cavalry at Fort Sam Houston, Texas, where he requested reassignment to the fledgling aeronautical service. He received training at the U.S. Army aviation school at College Park, Maryland, and Palm Beach, Florida. His first duty assignments were with the 1st Aero Squadron at Texas City, Texas, then San Diego, California.

North Island, in San Diego Bay, was a perfect location for aviation training; low flat terrain, firm sand for soft landings, and no trees of any size. The first unified Army Signal Corps aviation school was established on North Island in December of 1912, and over the next six months, aircraft and aviation personnel arrived from various Army aviation schools all over the country. On Monday, November 24, 1913, Lt. Eric Ellington and Lt. Hugh Kelly prepared their Wright C Flyer for and early morning training flight. Kelly was in the student pilot's seat, and Ellington was next to him in the instructor's seat. Kelly started the engine, the plane gained speed and lifted up off the runway into the early morning light. After one circle around the field, Kelly turned the plane around and began a training maneuver where the engine is cut off, then restarted. As the Wright flyer descended to about 200 feet, one of the pilots restarted the engine, as was expected. However, the sudden start-up of the engine put the airplane into a steep dive, and as the pilots and mechanics on the ground watched in horror, they could see Lt. Kelly brace himself for impact as the plane dove out of view. Both flyers were killed. Lt. Ellington was laid to rest at home in North Carolina, in the Clayton City Cemetery. He was one of the first flying aces and had been a well-liked and respected aviator.[2]

Col. Ira Rader (1887-1958)

L-R Col. Ira Rader and Wife, Mrs. Walter H. Frank, Maj. Walter H. Frank, and daughter Hazel Frank, courtesy of Ellington 1918

Colonel Rader was born in Mayten, California, in 1887. He graduated from West Point on June 13, 1911. His first assignment after leaving the academy was with the Nineteenth Infantry as Second Lieutenant at Camp Jossman, Phillipine Islands. He was stationed there until January 4, 1912, when his regiment was moved to Fort William McKinley. He remained in the Philippines until June 14, 1912, when he was transferred to the Twenty-Fourth Infantry, and later ordered to Corregidor until September, 1914, when he returned to the United States. Flying appealed to the young officer and he was attached as a student aviator to the Signal Corps Aviation School, San Diego, California, to begin flying training. On July 14, 1915, he was rated as a Junior Military Aviator, and assigned to the Aviation Section of the Signal Corps as a First Lieutenant. Shortly afterward he was assigned to the First Aero Squadron, at Fort Sill, Oklahoma. He served there until November 17, 1915. He was transferred to San Antonio, Texas, November 25, 1915. He served at the Aviation Post, Fort Sam Houston, until the border wars with Mexico began.

On March 11, 1915, he was ordered into Mexico with the First Aero Squadron as part of General Pershing's Punitive Expedition. He was attached to General Pershing's Headquarters from March 19, 1915, to September 20, 1916. Lt. Rader flew many sorties over the border into Mexico. On July 1, 1916, he was ordered to Mineola, New York, where he taught at the Signal Corps Aviation School until July 20, 1917. On May 16, 1917, he was promoted to Captain and made Departmental Aeronautical Officer, of the Central Department, Chicago, Illinois, and served from July 28 until October 13, 1917. He sailed for France soon afterward, arriving at Brest, France, November 12, 1917. He was briefly attached to Headquarters, Chief of Air

Service, Paris, and then assumed command of the Seventh Aviation Instruction Center, Clermont-Ferrand, France, on November 27, 1917. This command he held until September 11, 1918. On September 13, 1918, he was promoted to Lieutenant-Colonel, Air Service, and attached to the First Bombardment Group at Amanty, France. He engaged in active service over the lines during the St. Mihiel and Champagne attacks. He was on temporary duty at Headquarters, Air Service, S.O.S., Tours, France.

He sailed for the United States as Special Representative of Training Department, Air Service, on October 9, 1918. He served briefly at the Office of Director of Military Aeronautics, until November 2, 1918, until he was posted more permanently to Ellington Field, Texas.

On November 4, 1918, Lieutenant-Colonel Rader arrived at Ellington Field, succeeding Major Walter H. Frank as Commanding Officer. Through the years, he served in the Air Service, Air Corps, and finally the United States Air Force, from which he retired July 31, 1947. He died September 14, 1958 in North Carolina, and is buried in Arlington National Cemetery.

Lt. Granville Gutterson

Granville "Granny" Gutterson was born in Blue Earth County, Minne sota on April 9, 1897, to Gilbert and Alma Gutterson.[3] . Granny was an athlete of unusual ability, excelling in basketball and football, but not even the financial inducements offered to him could defy his inner sense of service and loyalty which drove him to do his part in the struggle for freedom overseas. Only what he considered the most hazardous branch of the service- the Army Air Corps- would satisfy his fearless spirit. While waiting for his "call up", he entered the University of Minnesota, became president of his class, made the freshman football Team and was pledged to Beta Theta Pi.

Cadet Gutterson entered the service December 12, 1917, and was sent to Ground School at Austin Texas. He graduated from there in January of 1918, and was assigned to the first class of the new bombing school Ellington Field, Texas. He graduated from bombardier school in May of 1918, and was commissioned as a Second Lieutenant May 25, 1918. He performed very well, and after completing the course, was asked to stay on as a Military Instructor, which was a testament to his skill and intelligence, but a crushing blow to his personal desire to get overseas as soon as possible and join his friends in fighting an air war. He waited every month for his orders overseas.

Granville met with every success in his military career and was rapidly promoted through the ranks. He enlisted as a first class private but within six months became a cadet, and then a commissioned officer. One month later he was assigned as one of the officers in charge of training. He diligently applied his mind to the job at hand, but his heart longed to "get across the ocean" and serve in the war in Europe with his buddies. He never met that goal. He finally received his overseas orders very late in the war, on Nov. 7, 1918, and he quickly packed up his gear in San Leon, Texas and headed for New York to ship out. The armistice was signed only a few days later, on November 11, and his overseas orders were cancelled before he even reached New York. After joining in the celebrations on the streets of New York and visiting his family in Philadelphia, there was nothing for Lt. Gutterson to do but wait and see what the government was going to do with its now-surplus flyers. He went to dances, visited friends, and played football, where he broke his ankle. He was put into the hospital for a few days, until it was decided the "break' was only bad sprain. He received orders to go back to San Leon, Texas, on November, 25th . He started his journey back with a bad cold and a sprained ankle. The last entry in his diary reads' "I haven't the least idea what the Govt. will do with me, and care less! A number of the boys in that first class of bombers have been shot down and are now pushing up daisies in France- and as long as I live, I'll never get over having regrets because I was not with them…I sure wish the armistice hadn't been signed *just yet.*"[4] J.A. Norton, Granny's high school teacher and athletic coach, added the following end note to the diary,

When he reached St. Louis, his condition made it necessary to consult a physician, who told him that if he went on to Texas he would be gambling with death. Granny's reply was 'My orders read Ellington Field.' …he collapsed as he was entering the Ellington Hospital. Hospital officials notified his parents of his serious condition, and Granny himself soon realized that the odds were against him…he gave detailed instructions to a fellow officer as to the disposal of his effects. He then dictated a farewell letter to his mother[5]

Alma Gutterson reached her son in the late evening of December 3rd, and remained with him through the night. 2nd Lt. Granville Gutterson died in the service of his country December 4, 1918, one of the thousands of victims of the influenza pandemic.

Col. Walter H. Reid, circa 1940. Taken from Army Air Force Training Command.

Col. Walter H. Reid (1890-1958)

Walter H. Reid was born in Harrison County, Missouri in May of 1890[11], to Abraham M. and Elizabeth Reid of Lincoln Township. By 1900, the complete Reid family consisted of father Abraham, mother Elizabeth, Thomas C., Walter H., and Jesse B.

The Reid family was living in Bethany, Missouri, in 1898, when the Spanish-American War was being fought. Smitten with the flame of patriotism, young Walter Reid took his air rifle and marchedinto the woods near his home to fight fought imaginary battles with the Spaniards.[12] At the age of fourteen, his enthusiasm for being a "fighting man" pushed him to lie about his age and enlist in the Missouri National Guard. In 1917, when the Army called for volunteers during World War I, he immediately joined the Army and was stationed at Camp Stanley, near San Antonio, Texas. He was commissioned as a First Lieutenant in the Cavalry, but was asked by the Army to transfer to the new Army Air Corps.[13] He was next stationed at Kelly Field, San Antonio, where he took the advanced flying course, and then in March 1918, Lt. Reid was transferred to Ellington Field, Texas. There he finished his Air Corps training with bombardment and gunnery courses.

After completing his coursework, Lt. Reid was transferred to Chanute Field, Illinois, then back to Kelly Field, Texas, and finally to the

Mexican-American border to fight the border wars. In 1920 he returned to Ellington Field where he served from 1920-1922 as a member of the First Pursuit Group.[14] During the next four years, Lt. Reid served tours of duty at Selfridge Field, Michigan, at an engineering school in Dayton, Ohio, and three years in Panama. He was reassigned to Ellington Field from 1926-August of 1931, serving first as an instructor and then commander of the 111th Observation Squadron of the Texas National Guard.[15] It was during this third tour of duty at Ellington Field that Reid met and married Miss Dorothy Ennis Cherry, daughter of Dillon B. and Emma Richardson Cherry, of Houston. After their marriage in 1927, the Reids lived in the Rice House, the Cherry's historic two-story colonial home located at 608 Fargo Avenue in Houston.[16]

In 1940, Col. Reid returned for his fourth tour of duty at Ellington Field. He served there as base commander for most of World War II. On April 10, 1944, he was transferred to temporary duty at San Angelo, Texas, as acting wing commander of the Thirty-fourth Flying Training Wing.[17] His subsequent permanent assignment in May of 1944, was to the advanced navigation school at Selman Field, Louisiana. In September of 1945, he was transferred to Randolph Field, Texas to be the Commanding Officer.[18] In June of 1946, Col. Walter Reid was awarded the Army's Legion of Merit for "Outstanding Organizational Ability" for his work at Ellington Field. A newspaper article pointed out that "...under Colonel Reid's able leadership, Ellington Field rose to the height of efficiency and produced a flow of pilots, bombardiers and navigators urgently needed for the successful prosecution of the war."[19]

Col Reid became the manager of the Aviation Department of the Houston Chamber of Commerce in February of 1949, after his retirement from the Army. He worked hard to promote and develop the addition of a second airport in Houston, and was appointed as the first Aviation Director of the Houston Municipal Airport in November by Mayor Roy Hofheinz in November, 1953. He served as Director until his resignation on January 1, 1955.[20] He died in Houston, Texas on December 7, 1958, leaving his wife, Dorothy, son Walter B., grandson Walter J., and his brothers Jesse B. and Thomas C. Reid.[21] Mrs. Reid died February 10, 1970.

Col. K. K. Black, courtesy of Kathryn Black Morrow Collection

Col. Kermit Kellogg Black (1907-1983)

My father was born in Adamsville, Alabama, in 1907. He began his military career when he was in highschool in Tampa, Florida. It was also at this time that he became interested in a relatively new and growing industry called Radio Communications. He constructed and operated his own Spark Gap transmitter and receivers, starting off with Crystal and Cat Whisker (Galena) detectors, before radio tubes were invented. He built and sold many receivers to neighbors and nearby residents. He was a young man with a young man's dreams, and on one occasion he traded one of his hand-built receivers for an 18-foot boat and motor, which he used for the next several years to fish the abundant lakes and streams around Tampa. Later he traded the boat and motor for a Model T. Ford Touring car which he used for hunting in the Florida Everglades.

In January of 1924, he enlisted in the 116th Horse Drawn Field Artillery Unit of the Florida National Guard. During the next several years he spent so much time on a horse for the National Guard and his college Reserve Officers Training Corps (R.O.T.C) unit, that in his 1929 college yearbook he was nominated to the Hall of Fame with the quote "K. K. Black—fortunately for him the horseflies don't live all year."[6]

When he entered the University of Florida in the fall of 1925 to study Engineering, radio was a new and rapidly developing field. Radio broadcasting came to the University of Florida campus in 1928, and my father and Walter L. "Red" Barber (1908-1992) were appointed as the initial team of studio announcers for the campus station, WRUF. Red Barber was so excited about being in front of a microphone that he dropped out of college and eventually became a well-known radio announcer. Red was most remembered as a sports announcer, and was the voice of the Brooklyn Dodgers for many years.[7]

When the Great Depression hit Florida, it forced an early end to my father's college education. However, he continued his military career as a member of the Reserve Officers Training Corps (R.O.T.C.) in Florida, worked at radio station WMBR in Tampa, and occupied the remainder of his time by pursuing his interest in two other new and exciting fields- flying and aerial photography. Aerial photography jobs turned into flying lessons, which were taken with the pilots of the famous barnstorming group, "The Gates Flying Circus". One of those pilots was a young man named Charles A. Lindbergh, who later became the first man to fly solo across the Atlantic Ocean. The type of aircraft used for stunt flying and lessons in those days was the same aircraft used at Ellington Field during World War I, the JN 4 or "Jenny." After training in the Jennys, Kermit's first solo flight , as well as his first "dead stick" landing, was made in an Alexander Eaglerock bi-plane with an OX-5 engine.

In May of 1929, he was commissioned as a 2nd Lieutenant in the Infantry Officers Reserve Corps, U.S. Army and subsequently assigned to Fort Sam Houston, Texas. In September of the same year, he left Tampa, Florida and went to work for the Houston Lighting and Power Company. In 1931 he was transferred to Anti-Aircraft Artillery and his Army Reserve assignments moved him to several different units in Texas. He served as Commanding Officer of the Civilian Conservation Corps (C.C.C.) in Woden and Huntsville, Texas, from 1935-1937.

In the spring of 1946 he was released from active duty and returned to his civilian occupation as President of the Navigation Instrument Company, located at 4800 Clinton Drive near the Houston ship channel. An article in the University of Houston campus newspaper, "The Cougar" dated October, 1947, reported that Mr. K.K. Black, President of the Navigation Instrument Company, had donated a large and expensive piece of radar equipment to the University, which he hoped would be used for teaching radar applications and perhaps would inspire further development of radar technology.[8] This site of the Navigation Instrument Company later became part of the main campus for Brown and Root construction company (later Kellogg, Brown and Root).

As the United States prepared to enter World War II, my father was called to active duty in December of 1940. He served six years on active duty with the Coast Artillery Reserve in Houston from 1940-1946 and was released to return to his civilian job as President of the Navigation

Instrument Company in Houston. In 1951, he was called back into active duty as a member of the newly created Air Force[9], with the rank of Colonel, and assigned as the Commander of the 158th Aircraft Control and Warning Group, formed at Ellington Air Force Base. Col. Black was the Director of Materiel, Continental Airways and Air Communications from 1954 through 1960, and received an Air Force Commendation Medal as a result of his achievements and performance in managing the communications and equipment for the United States Air Force. Col. Black retired in 1963, after more than thirty-nine years of military service. He and his wife Evangeline (Vee) McPherson Black lived in Midwest City, Oklahoma, near Tinker Air Force Base. Col. Black died in 1983.[10]

George W. Bush (1946-Still Living)

1st Lt. George W. Bush at the Air National Guard hangar, Ellington Air Force Base, Texas, circa 1970, courtesy of 147th FIG Photo Gallery online

Texas Governor, then United States President, George W. Bush was an F-102 pilot with the Texas Air National Guard at Ellington Field from 1968-1973, in the 147th FIG. As a member of the unit, Lt. Bush flew the supersonic F-102 Delta Dagger. George W. Bush, the son of George H. W. and Barbara Bush, grew up in Midland and Houston, Texas. He received a bachelor's degree from Yale University and an MBA from Harvard University, then returned to Texas. He formed Bush Exploration, an oil exploration company in Midland, Texas, and ran for Congress. He later became the managing general partner of the Texas Rangers Baseball Team. As a theme for the Governor's Inauguration, Bush chose "What Texans Can Dream, Texans Can Do," a reflection of his belief in individual potential and citizen involvement in the community.

At Bush's Gubernatorial Inauguration on January 17, 1995, a flying formation of F-16s roared through the skies over Austin, flown by Texans of the 111th Fighter /Squadron of the 147th Fighter Interceptor Group of the Texas Air National Guard from Ellington Field, to honor of one of their own. A marching unit comprised of forty men and women from Ellington marched in the inaugural parade through the streets of Austin.[22] Bush was elected President of the United States in 2000, and re-elected in 2004. It was a significant point of pride to his National Guard "family" of the 147th Fighter Interceptor Group at Ellington Field, Texas, that one of their own achieved the highest office in the United States.

Lt. George W. Bush getting his Lieutenant's bars pinned on by his father, George H. W. Bush, November, 1970, at Ellington Air Force Base, Texas, courtesy of 147th FIG Photo Gallery online

End Notes

[1] Clayton Chronicle, October 11, 1917, as quoted in *Ellington Field: a Short History, 1917-1963,* by Erik Carlson.

[2] Erik Carlson, *Ellington Field: A Short History, 1917-1963.* NASA/CR-19999-208921. February, 1999, pp. 5-12.

[3] 1900 Census, Blue Earth County, Minnesota.

[4] Gutterson, 170.

[5] Gutterson, 173.

[6] University of Florida Yearbook, "The Seminole", 1929, p. 362.

[7] Radio Hall of Fame, Sportscasters, www.radiohof.org/sportscasters/redbarber.html. Accessed 9/17/03.

[8] Dan Hardy. "All Ears", *The Cougar*, October 3, 1947.

[9] The United States Air Force was created as a separate branch of the military on July 26, 1947, as part on the National Security Act. Gen. Carl A. Spaatz became the first Chief of Staff, with W. Stuart Symington as Secretary of the Air Force.... The new Air Force was fortunate to have these two men as its first leaders. They regarded air power as an instrument of national policy and of great importance to national defense.... Air Force 50th Anniversary site, www.airforcehsitory.hq.af.mil/soi/index.htm. Accessed 12/2/2001.

[10] Personal papers of Col. K.K. Black in the possession of daughter, Kathryn K. Morrow, 2005

[11] 1900 Census, Lincoln County, Missouri. Transcription courtesy of Les Beeks, Missouri GenWeb project researcher, May 2005.

[12] *Houston Post,* January 5, 1941.

[13] *Houston Press,* October 29, 1941.

[14] Ibid., *Houston Post,* April 5,1941,

[15] *Houston Press,* October 29, 1941

[16] 1930 United States Census, ED 99, p. 254. Head of household, Dillon B. Cherry.

[17] *The Houston Post,* November 25, 1953.

[18] *The Houston Post, June 30, 1946.*

[19] Ibid.

[20] *The Houston Post,* December 22, 1955.

[21] *The Houston Post*, December 9, 1958.

[22] Gubernatorial Press Release, March 5, 1995. Copy courtesy of the Base Historian's Office, Ellington Field, Texas.

Appendixes, Bibliography & Indexes

Appendix One

Unless they appear elsewhere in the book, names in these appendices are not included in the index, since they are listed alphabetically here. These appendices are intended to give recognition to two groups of citizens who were often overlooked during World War II, or tolerated only out of necessity; the women, and the African Americans. They were also an important part of the effort to "Keep 'Em Flying."

First Graduating Class Roster
Women's Flight Training Detachment (WFTD) Class 43-1

(Married name in brackets if known)

Boysen, Eleanor (Morgan)
Brown, G.C. (Kindig)
Callighan, Claire G.
Colber, Mary Lou (Neale)
Collins, Edna C. (Kingdon)
Granger, Byrd Howell
Gray, Marjorie W.
Greenblatt, Evelyn S. (Howren)
Hellman, Ruth K.
Johnson, Ann R.
Johnson, Vega
Ketcham, Marjorie J. (Deacon)
Kumler, Marjorie
Lamphere, Marylene Geraldine (Nyman)
Mackey, Marion (deGregorio)
McCormick, Margaret E.
McKinley, Elizabeth A (Matray)
Miller, Sidney
Richards, Lovelle (Benesh)
Staughan, Jane S.
Tackaberry, Betty C. (Blake)
Tacke, Magda T.
Young, Dorothy L

Appendix Two

Members of the 788TH Women's Army Corps (WAC)
Ellington Field, 1943

Bain, Capt. Louise E., Commanding Officer
Boyd, 1st Lt. Helen W., Assistant Operations Officer
Sewell, 2nd Lt. Emily E, Adjutant and Supply Officer

Allen, Evelyn M., Cpl.
Atlas, Rose, Cpl.
Baker, Virginia L,. Cpl.
Berry, Merlene, Pvt. 1C
Blalock, Emma D., Cpl.
Cebula, Josephine, Cpl.
Cooke Evelyn F., Cpl.
Cullen, Jean I., First Sgt.
Cushman, B.H., Cpl.
Day, G.J., Cpl.
Degogorza, Beatriz M., Pvt. 1C
Dorchak, Marie A., Cpl.
Dumond, Frances, Cpl.
Dziubinski, Irene M., Cpl.
Eaton, Mary C., Cpl.
Eshee, Barbara I., Pvt. 1C
Fernekes, Camille C., Pvt. 1C
Finley, Marion P., Pvt. 1C
Fisher, Victoria T., Pvt. 1C.
Friend, Donna M., Cpl.
Gray, Class Ruth A ,Pvt. 1sr.
Grubbs, S.L., Pvt. 1C
Hafer, Rue E., Cpl.
Hager, Ellen K., Pvt. 1C
Holaus, Margaret W., Pvt. 1C
Howden, Eileen P., Pvt. 1C
Jacko, Margaret I., Cpl.
Jakupcin, Helen, Pvt. 1C
Jennings, Vera O., Pvt. 1C
Kaiser, Nina K., Cpl.
Knapp, Mary F,. Pvt. 1C.
Kurtzhals, Mary T., Cpl.
Lambert, Jean M., Pvt. 1C
Lytle, Anna M,. Pvt. 1C
Malde, Fern M., Pvt. 1C
Manciocchi, Margaret, Cpl.
Martin, Willie D., Cpl.
McConnon, Helen V., Cpl.
McDonald, Frances A, Cpl.
McRae, Irene M., Pvt. 1C
Miller, Jessie L., Pvt. 1C
Neustaetter, Deborah S., Pvt. 1C
Northern, Alma G., Sgt.
Ostrander, Doretta K., Cpl.
O'Sullivan, Virginia, Pvt. 1C
Palmer, Esther C, Pvt. 1C
Pavlovsky, Marian, Pvt. 1C
Polim, Ricky, Sgt.
Polk, Lydia, Pvt. 1C
Quinn, Mary, Cpl.
Roads, Ellen L., Sgt.

Sherwood, Anita F., Sgt.
Stannard, Joyce M, Staff Sgt.
Stevens, Elizabeth, Sgt.
Whitecraft, Thelma M., Pvt. 1C
Willis, Sarah L., Pvt.
Wold, Mildred E., Staff Sgt.

Appendix Three

79TH Aviation Squadron

Commanding Officer—Captain Bernard H. Rogers
Adjutant—Captain Seaborn Jones
Supply Officer—First Lieutenant Adrian L. Schroeder

More information, including photographs of all of these men and en listment records for some of these men can be obtained by contacting the author.

Alexander, Lewis E.,Pvt.
Alexander, Samuel B., Pvt
Allen, Pvt 1st C
Allen, Roosevelt, Pvt
Attley, Wickliffe, Pvt 1st
Austin, Birlen, Pvt.
Bacon, Claude W., Pvt. 1st C
Barner, Looney, Pvt
Barnes, Booker T, Pvt.
Barr, Luther, Pvt 1st C
Barrett, Morris, Pvt
Battist, Frank, Pvt
Beaufort, Butler L,Pvt.1stC
Belk, Johnnie, Pvt.
Bell, Freddie, Cpl
Bentley, Martin,Pvt 1stC
Berry, Clarence, Pvt
Bessard, Felix H., Pvt
Borders, James, Cpl
Bowens, Preston. Pvt
Bowie, Joseph, Cpl
Boyd, Willie, Pvt
Bradley, Murphy, Pvt.
Branch, Willie, Cpl
Brewer, Henry T., Pvt 1st C
Brown, Johnnie W., Cpl.
Brown, Christ, Pvt. 1st C
Bryant, Mack, Pvt 1st C
Bryant, Robert M., Pvt.
Bullock,Sylvester, Cpl.
Burge, Lazarus, Pvt
Burton, Isaiah, Pvt
Cains, Reed, Cpl.
Calliham, Roy, Pvt.
Carlton, Edward E., Cpl.
Carmouche, Elmo L., Cpl

Carr, Sullivan, Pvt
Carr, Vernon H., Staff Sgt.
Carrier, Wilbert, Pvt 1st C
Carswell, James, Pvt.
Carter, Charles W., Sgt.
Chachere, Willie, Pvt
Clark, Levie, Pvt.
Clayborne, James L., Pvt 1st C
Clark, Sandis, Pvt. 1st C
Cleveland, Isaac, Pvt 1st C
Colar, Sylvanus W., Pvt
Cole, Houston, Pvt. 1st C
Coleman, James E , Sgt.
Conley, Rufus C., 1st Sgt.
Cooks, John B., Pvt
Cooper, Joseph, Pvt
Cotton, Fred, Cpl.
Cotton, Moses, Pvt
Cousin, Sylvester, Pvt.
Cox, Roy, Pvt.
Crooms, Henry M., Cpl
Dabney, Thomas, Pvt
Daniels, Searcy, Pvt
Davis, Frank, Pvt 1st C
Davison, Lee R., Pvt.
Deboise, Johnnie, Pvt
Deransburg, Horace C., Sgt.
Dorsey, Henry M., Pvt 1st C
Felix, Mark, Pvt. 1st C
Flakes, Sylvester, Pvt.
Flix, Raphael H., Sgt.
Fondal, Edward R., Pvt
Francis, Hazely, Pvt 1st C
Francis, Horace, Pvt. 1st C
Frank, Johnnie L., Pvt
Frederick, William S., Pvt 1st C
Freeman, Robert, Cpl.
Gaines, Joseph N., Cpl.
Ganier, Rene, Pvt.
Garner, Albert, Pvt 1st C
Gatling, Luther E., Sgt.
Gay, Guthrie, Sgt.
Gibbs, Ernest C., Sgt.
Glen, George, Pvt
Glover, Albert, Pvt.
Goffney, Edgar, Pvt
Gosserand, Fred, Pvt
Green, George, Pvt.
Greenleaf, Johnnie B., Pvt.
Greer, Earnest, Pvt. 1st C
Gross, Arthur A., Pvt 1st C
Hair, J.B., Sgt.
Hall, John W., Pvt 1st
Harris, Charles C., Pvt
Harris, John, jr., Pvt
Holmes, Drafford, Pvt. 1st C
Horton. Theodore, Pvt 1st C
Hosey,Hudson, Pvt 1st C
Hutchison, Thomas J., Pvt.
Andrew L., Staff Sgt.
Jack, Samuel, Pvt. 1st C
Jackson, Alvin, Pvt 1st C
Jackson, Ranel, Cpl.
Jean Louis, John C., Pvt
Jemison William Cpl.
Jenkins Orville B. Pvt 1st C
Johnson Overton Pvt.
Johnson Phillip Pvt
Johnson Warren A. Pvt
Jones, Fred Pvt.
Jones, Sam Pvt. 1st C
Jones, Samuel Pvt 1st C
Joseph, Frank Pvt
Ladner, Cornelius A., Staff Sgt.

Lamply Thearon Pvt.
Lancelin, Joseph J. Pvt 1st C
Laymond, Laney G. Jr. Cpl.
Lee, John D. Pvt. 1st C
Lefrere, Percy P. Cpl.
Legras, Ignatius J., Cpl.
Lewis, L.E., Cpl.
Lewis, Odell, Pvt
Love, Norfolk, Pvt 1st C
Major, Isaiah, Pvt.
Martin, Isaiah, Pvt
Martin, Lionel, Cpl.
Mason, Ben, Pvt.
Mathis, Alexander, Pvt 1st C
Matthews, Earl, Cpl.
McGary, Norman, Pvt. 1st C
McGuire, Eugene, Pvt
McKinnon, Snowden L, Tech Sgt
Menard, Joseph, Pvt
Miles, Johnny, Pvt
Mingleton, Joe J., Pvt.
Nellon, Edward, jr., Pvt
Norton, Neal G., Pvt 1st C
Ordogne, Robert, Pvt. 1st C
Owens, George, Cpl.
Parent, Nelson G., jr, Cpl.
Pearson, James, Pvt.
Peordin, Ferdinand, Pvt
Plummer, Walter, Pvt
Porter, Archie, Cpl.
PrioleauDouglasCpl.
Reed, Leard Pvt.
Rhone, Willie, Jr. Cpl.
Richards, Forest Pvt
Richards, Jimmie Pvt.
Richardson, James, jr., Pvt 1st C
Richardson, Leslie, Pvt
Riley, Nathaniel Pvt 1st C
Roberson, Leslie E. Pvt
Roberson, Lewis Pvt. 1st C
Robertson, Sheade Pvt 1st C
Ross, Norman B., Pvt.
Royal, Samuel L. Pvt.
Russell, William O. Sgt.
Schummpert, Frank Pvt
Schweder, Alberta E., Cpl.
Smith, John Z. Pvt
Smith, Robert W, Pvt 1st C
Snearl, Allen Cpl.
Stevenson, Frank Pvt.
Stewart, Beaufort F. Sgt.
Stewart,. Edward Pvt
Stewart, Joshua N. Cpl.
Sylvester, Antwine, Pvt.
Talley, George H. Pvt. 1st C
Taylor, Arthur A. Cpl.
Taylor, Edward Pvt
Taylor, Isaiah J. Pvt
Terrance, Alvin Pvt.
Thibodeaux, Patrick W., Cpl.
Thurman, Ruben Pvt
Tolliver, Ulysses Sgt.
Tousant, Isadore Pvt.
Turner, Jessie R. Pvt
Ventress, Sam Pvt 1st C
Waddy, Gastonia Pvt
Walker, Iry Pvt.
Wallace,Birtell Pvt.
Walls, James Cpl.
Webb, Jackson, Staff Sgt.
White, Coleman, Cpl.
Williams, Lee, Pvt. 1st C
Williams, Leroy, Pvt
Woods, Clarence, Pvt 1st C

Bibliography

Archives and Collections

Air Force History and Research Agency (AFHRA), Maxwell Air Force Base, Montgomery, Alabama.

Album of Station Information, Ellington Field, Texas. Maxwell AFB: AFHRA, 2002. Microfilm, roll B2175.

Fyfe, Lt. Joseph S. *History of the Station Hospital at Ellington Field, Texas, 21 May 1941-7 December 1941* (Maxwell AFB: AFHRA, 2002), Microfilm, roll B2175, Havins, Lt. T. R.

The History of Ellington Field, April 1941-1 March 1944, 2 vols. Maxwell AFB: AFRHA, 2002. Microfilm, roll B 2175.

History of the 2517th Base Unit, 1May-30 June 1945. Maxwell AFB: AFHRA, 2002. Microfilm, roll B2175

History of the 2517th Base Unit, 1 September-31 October 1945. Maxwell AFB: AFHRA, 2002. Microfilm, roll B2175.

History of the 2517th Base Unit, 1 November-31 December 1945. Maxwell AFB: AFHRA, 2002. Microfilm, roll B2175

Bain, Louise E. *History of the AAF WAC Detachment, Ellington Field, Texas, 1 March 1944 —1 May 1944.* Maxwell AFB: AFRHA, 2002. Microfilm, roll B 2175.

History of the Pilot School, Ellington Field, Texas, 1940-1 March 1944. Maxwell AFB: AFRHA), 2002. Microfilm, roll B 2175.

History of the 619th and 711th Army Bands. Maxwell AFB: Air Force History and Research Archives (AFRHA), 2002. Microfilm, roll B 2175.

Base Historian's Office, Ellington Field, Texas, Various, mostly one page base and unit histories, press release drafts, notes and articles, many written or edited by Margaret Houghton, Secretary to the Base Commander's Office.

Houghton, Margaret. *History of Ellington Air Force Base,* dated Oct 23, 1951.

Public Information Office, Ellington Air Force Base. *The Mission and Manner of Execution of Ellington Air Force Base, Houston, Texas,* dated April 27, 1951, 1, 2.

Johnson Space Center History Collection (JSC), University of Houston Clear Lake Archives, Houston, Texas.

Aldrich, Roy C. Interview by Robert B. Merrifield, October 22, 1968. Transcript. JSC.

Bell Aerosystems Company News Bureau, New York, January 20, 1967. Press Release.
Byrnes, Martin, jr. Interview by Robert B. Merrifield, December 12, 1967. Transcript. JSC.
Gilruth, Robert R. to Dr. George E. Mueller. Letter. June 12, 1968. JSC.
Gilruth, Robert R. Letter. August 10, 1971. JSC.
Grimm, Dean Franklin. Interview by Carol Butler, August 17, 2000. Transcript. JSC.
Holzapfel, Richard H. NASA Safety Engineer. Memorandum dated May 7, 1968. JSC.
Hjornevik, Wesley L. Interview by Robert L. Merrifield March 9, 1967. Transcript. JSC.
Johnson Space Center Announcement, March 16, 1989. JSC.
Lang, Dave W. Interview by Robert B. Merrifield, December 12, 1967. Transcript. JSC.
Lang, Dave W. *The Impact of The Manned Spacecraft Center on the Houston Gulf Coast Area.*
Houston: National Aeronautics and Space Administration, 1967. JSC.
McLeaish, John E. Interview by Rebecca Wright, Nov. 15, 2001. Transcript. JSC.
Space News Roundup, Johnson Space Center History Collection, University of Houston Clear Lake Archives, Houston, Texas, September 1, 1972 to October 25, 1991.

General Reference

Books

Alexander, Thomas E. *The Wings of Change. The Army Air Force Experience in Texas During World War II.* McWhiney Foundation Press, Abilene, 2003.
Army Air Forces Training Command, Ellington Field, Texas. Baton Rouge: Army and Navy Publishing Company of Louisiana, c. 1942.
Bilstein, Roger, and Jay Miller. *Aviation in Texas.* San Antonio: Texas Monthly Press, 1985.
Dalfiume, Richard M. *Desegregation of the U.S. Armed Forces:Fighting on Two Fronts 1939-1953,*Columbia: University of Missouri Press, 1969.
Daso, Dik Alan. *Hap Arnold and the Evolution of American Airpower.* Washington: Smithsonian Institution Press, 2000.
Ellington Air Force Base, Aircraft Observer Training. Army & Navy Publishing Company, Inc. Baton Rouge, LA, 1956.
Foner, Jack H. *Blacks and the Military in American History.* New York: Praeger Publishers, 1974.
Graves, Celeste, *A View From The Doghouse of the 319th AAFWTD.* Bloomington: AuthorHouse, 2004.
Greene, Robert Ewell. *Black Defenders of America, 1773-1973.* Chicago: Johnson Publishing Company, Inc., 1974.
Greenfield, Kent Roberts, ed. *United States Army in World War II.* Vol. 6, *The Technical Services.* Part 5, *The Signal Corps:The Emergency,* by Dulaney Terrett. Washington D.C.: Office of the Chief of Military History, Department of the Army, 1956.
Greenfield, Kent Roberts, ed. *United States Army in World War II.* Vol. 8, *Special Studies.*

Part 7, *Buying Aircraft: Materiel Procurement for the Army Air Forces* by Irving Brinton. Holley, Jr.. Washington D.C.: Office of the Chief of Military History, Department of the Army, 1956.

Gutterson, Gilbert. *Granville, Tales and Tailspins From A Flyer's Diary.* New York: The Abingdon Press, 1919.

Hacker, Barton C, and James M. Grimwood. *On the Shoulders of Titans. A History of Project Gemini.* Washington, D.C.: Scientific and Technical Office, National Aeronautics and Space Administration, 1997.

Hardy, Dan. *The Cougar.* Houston: University of Houston,_October 3, 1947.

Haynes, Robert V., *A Night of Violence: The Houston Riot of 1917* (Baton Rouge: Louisiana State University Press, 1976).

WPA Writers Program, *Houston* (Houston: Anson Jones, 1942).

Isserman, Maurice and Michael Kazin. *America Divided: the Civil War of the 1960's.* New York: Oxford University Press, 2000.

Johnston, Marguerite. *Houston, the Unknown City, 1836-1946.* College Station: Texas A&M University Press, 1994.

Mandelbaum, David. *Soldier Groups and Negro Soldiers.* Berkeley: University of California Press, 1952.

Navigation School, Ellington Air Force Base 1950.(Baton Rouge: A&N Pictorial Publishers, 1950.

Nichols. Lee. *Breakthrough On the Color Front.* New York: Random House Publishers, 1954.

Noggle, Anne. *For God, Country and the Thrill of It: Women Airforce Service pilots in World War II.* College Station: Texas A&M University Press, 1990.

Payne, Charles M. *I've Got the Light of Freedom.* Berkeley: University of California Press, 1995.

Rutherford, William A. "Jim Crow: a Problem in Diplomacy," *The Nation, 175. (November 8, 1952).*

Sherry, Michael S. *In the Shadow of War: The United States Since the 1930's.* New Haven*: Yale University Press, 1995.*

Stack, Lt. Joe. *Ellington 1918.* Houston: Private Printing, 1918.

Seminole, 1929. H.D. Aikin, Editor in Chief, Marry A. Carlton Managing Editor. Gainesville: University of Florida Press, 1929.

Truman, Harry S. M*emoirs.* Garden City: Doubleday & Company, Inc. 1955-1956, 2 volumes.

Warnock, A. Timothy. *Air Power Versus U-Boats: Confronting Hitler's Submarine Menace in the European Theater.* Washington, D.C.: Air Force History and Museums Program, 1999.

Wiggins, Melanie. *Torpedoes in the Gulf: Galveston and the U-Boats, 1942-1943.*College Station: Texas A&M University Press, 1995.

Yohalem, Alice and Quentin B. Ridgely. *Desegregation and Career Goals: Children of Air Force Families.* Praeger Studies in U.S Economic, Social, and Political Issues. New York: Praeger Publishers, 1974.

Government Publications

"Astronaut Program-Applications Chart, also Minority and Women Astronauts Selected-Through 2000 Chart," NASA Public Relations Department, 2003.

"Charles E. Yeager Biography". Edwards Air Force Base: Office of Public Affairs, 1993.

City of Houston, *Ellington Field Master Plan Study.* Vol. 1 & 2, Bedford, New Hampshire: Hoyle, Tanner & Associates, Inc., 1987.

City of Houston. *1998 Economic Impact Study, Houston Airport System.* Houston: City of Houston, 1998.

Department of the Air Force, Office of Information Services, A Chronology of American Aerospace Events, Washington, 1959.

Ellington Field Master Plan Update, Site Suitability Analysis. San Francisco: Leigh Fisher Associates, 2002.

Greater Houston Partnership, Research Department, *Houston Facts 2005.* Houston, 2005.

Hallett, George E.A. *Airplane Motors; A Course of Practical Instruction in Their Care and Overhauling for the Use of Military Aviators,* (Washington, Government Printing Office, 1917).

Shiner, John F. *The United States Air Force General Histories. Foulois and the U.S. Air Corps 1931-1935.* Washington D.C.: Office of Air Force History, United States Air Force, 1983.

"U.S. Signal Corps Agreement and Specifications for a Heavier-Than-Air Flying Machine," Specification No. 286, General Requirements Section, Paragraph 4

Unpublished Sources

Black, Col. K.K., USAF Retired. Personal Papers, Military Orders and Records, 1939-1981.

Black, Col. K.K. to Senator Olin Teague, April 14, 1958, in personal papers.

Carlson, Erik, *Ellington Field: A Short History, 1917-1963.* NASA A/CR-1999-208921, February 1999.

McNair, Ira B. Letters from Ellington Field 1918-1920. Xerox copies courtesy of grandson.

No Author. *Ellington Air Force Base.* Base History Office, Ellington Field [circa 1960].

Official Program For the Dedication of the Air Defense Control Center and Presentation of Battle Honors to the 158th Aircraft Warning Group. May 26, 1951,in personal papers of Col. K.K. Black.

William Lecel Lee Papers, 1927-69. Dwight D. Eisenhower Library, Abilene, Kansas. Accessions 71-59, 71-59/1, 72-35, 73-20 and 73-20/1.

No Author. *Historical Background—Ellington Air Force Base, Houston, Texas,* Houston Airport System Operations Office, Ellington Field [circa 1984].

Newspaper Articles

Austin American Statesman, March 20, 1989.

Berry, Michael. "Right Time, Place for Vets Museum at Ellington," *Houston Chronicle Outlook*, December 26, 2002.

Houston Chronicle, July 15, 1917.

Houston Chronicle, June 6, 1940—October 6, 1968.

Higgins, Jim. *Ellington Field 1917. Houston Chronicle Magazine*, Texas Section, November 1, 1987.

The Houston Post, April 4, 1941—July 13, 1950.

"Ellington Was Tents on Mud in '17, Cadet Then Recalls Here," *The Houston Post*, March 7, 1941.

Houston Press, August 24, 1917.

Houston Press, May, 1941-May 1942.

LaPorte Liberal, July 14, 1950.

Pittsburgh Courier, June 28, 1941.

Skylander, October 26, 1951

Press Releases

Gubernatorial Inauguration, March 5, 1995. Copy courtesy of the Base Historian's Office, Ellington Field, Texas.

Online Sources

Billings, Molly. *The Influenza Pandemic of 1918*, Stanford University Education Group, at www.stanford.edu/group/virus/uda.

"Danbury, Texas." Handbook of Texas Online website at www.tsha.utexas.edu/handbook/online/articles.

"Ellington Update", Lonestar Times, LonestarTimes.com, May 17. 2005.

"Establishing the President's Committee On Equality of Treatment and Opportunity in the Armed Forces," Executive Order No. 9981 dated July 26, 1948. At www.pbs.org/wgbh/annex/presidents/nf/resource/Truman.

"Evolution of the Department of the Air Force." Air Force History at www.airforcehistory.

"General Carl Spaatz, USAF, Retired." Department of Defense Office of Public Information, Press Branch. www.wpafb.af.mil/museum/afp/spaatz.

Interviews

Briggs, CMSGT Joe, interview by author, May 16, 2007.

Case, Mary. Ellington Airport Manager, Houston Airport System. Telephone interview by author, April 7,2003, Houston, Texas.

Jones, Col. Steve. Air National Guard 147TH Vice Flight Wing Commander at Ellington Field. Interview by Paul Pendergraft, tape recording, October 9, 2001, KUHF News, Houston, Texas.

Luna, Lt. Col. Bob. Military Public Affairs Officer, Texas National Guard at Ellington Field. Interview by Paul Pendergraft, tape recording, October 14, 2001, KUHF News, Houston, Texas.

McLemore, Dr. Kent, Assistant Deputy Director for Planning, Houston Airport System. Live interview by author March 12, 2003, Houston, Texas.

Radcliff, Vaughn. World Ward II soldier at Ellington Field. Telephone interview by author April 14, 2005, interview at his home April 26, 2005.

Ross, Duane L. Manager of Astronaut Candidate Selection and Training, Johnson Space Center. Telephone interviews by author, March 10, 2003, May 11, 2005, Houston, Texas.

Staudenmayer, Minta, Interview by author April 14, 2005. Houston, Texas.

Correspondence

Kincaid, Yvonne, email response, Yvonne.Kincaid@pentagon.af.mil, accessed 12/7/2001

Meridith, Msgt. Troy, to Kathryn Black Morrow, May 27, 2002 by email.

Miscellaneous

California Death Index, 1940-1990.

1880 Census, Harrison County, Missouri.

1900 Census, Harrison County, Missouri.

Lincoln Center Cemetery Records, Harrison County, Missouri.

1900 Census, Blue Earth County, Minnesota.

INDEXES

Names & Places

Note: The references to Ellington, Ellington Field and Ellington Air Force Base are too numerous in the book to list in the index. All other names and places will be listed once, but may appear more than once on the page. Names mentioned in the end notes that would not be listed in the bibliography are also included in this index.

— A —

— B —

— C —

— O —

— P —

— Q —

— R —

— S —

— T —

Subjects

Units

Note: The unit designations are typed as they were printed in the source material. When searching for a particular unit, look for a numerical name as well as a text name; 1st Aero Squadron and First Aero Squadron.

Aircraft